OTTERY ST MARY
A Devonshire Town

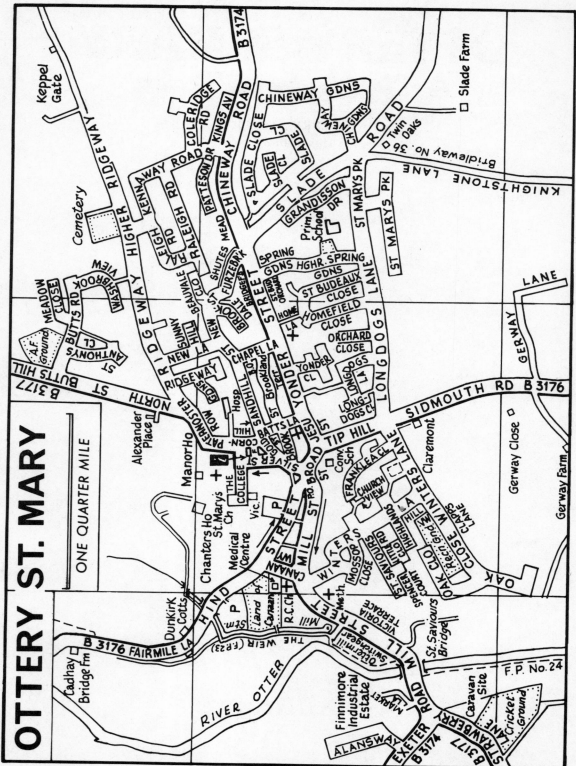

OTTERY ST. MARY

ONE QUARTER MILE

Frontispiece: Ottery St Mary, Street Plan (Drawn by John Yonge, Exeter)

OTTERY St MARY
A Devonshire Town

John A. Whitham

Out of monuments, names, words, proverbs, traditions, private records and evidence, fragments of stories, passages of books and the like, we doe save and recover somewhat from the deluge of time.

Francis Bacon
(1561-1626)

Phillimore

1984

Published by
PHILLIMORE & CO. LTD.
Shopwyke Hall, Chichester, Sussex

ISBN 0 85033 526 4

Printed and bound in Great Britain by
THE CAMELOT PRESS LTD
Southampton, England

CONTENTS

LIST OF PLATES

(between pages 18 and 19)

LIST OF TEXT ILLUSTRATIONS

Frontispiece: Ottery St Mary, Street plan

Proceeding from Exeter to Honiton, we were presented within six miles of Honiton, with the sweetest scene of cultivation I ever beheld. This may be called the garden of Devonshire.

The Rev Richard Polwhele in
A History of Devon (1797)
quoting an earlier writer

PREFACE

'Let us not rashly quit our hold upon the past'.—William Hazlitt (1778–1830)

THE STORY of any town or village is woven into the wider pattern of our national history, of which it forms an integral part. We are concerned with its people and development through the ages, and because of an inherent desire to know more about the place in which we live, much of absorbing interest may be discovered which might otherwise have lain dormant. If we are to gain an appreciation and understanding of any place or building, we must first learn something of its historical background—how it came to be on that particular site, and why it is so named.

Compiling a local history is rather like attempting to piece together a large jig-saw puzzle, for one is constantly searching for missing pieces. The discovery of some of these—often from unexpected sources—is gratifying, but there are always further gaps which remain to be filled in order to make our picture more complete.

Information has to be sought from a wide variety of sources ranging from old title deeds to newspaper 'cuttings', and these should be checked with the utmost care so as to ensure accuracy, for this is of vital importance. So often does one find some error or misconception blindly repeated from an unreliable source without attempting to check its accuracy.

Much useful information can be provided by old deeds and documents; for instance, reference is made in a deed dated 1762 to 'the Bridge near Tiphill foot' in Ottery St Mary. This was possibly over what was called Great Well Stream, which formerly flowed along the south side of Yonder Street and Jesu Street, and continued on into Mill Street. This has long since disappeared, but it was typical of many towns in Devon to find a stream running by the side of the street and spanned by a series of small bridges.

Unfortunately, many old deeds simply get tied in bundles and discarded as being of no further use, or, in some cases, the parchment finds its way to finish up as a lampshade!

The most informative source of local history is possibly to be found in antique maps and plans. The Tithe Map and Apportionment of 1842 is an invaluable parish survey, and provides details of land ownership, including the names of the occupiers of each property, together with the area, tithe-payment and type of cultivation. Field-names are also shown, which would in many cases otherwise have been forgotten. Professor F. W. Maitland in 1897, considered that 'two little fragments' of the One-inch Ordnance Map were 'more eloquent than would be many paragraphs of written discourse'.

xi

The parish registers of baptisms, marriages and burials are also of great value to the local historian, and provide much fascinating information. They tell us of old family names in the parish, throw light on the various occupations, provide some indication of population, and the incidence of plague and disease. The parish clerk would often enter notes on matters of local interest upon the flyleaf of the register, and we learn that in August 1748 '. . . great numbers of Eastern Locusts were seen in this County [Devon], and most parts of England'.

The preparation of this book has taken place over many years in response to a demand for a detailed history, and I have attempted so far as possible to deal with my subject chronologically, so as to present a continuous account of this corner of Devon from earliest times. Having lived at Ottery St Mary for nearly forty years, and with a life-long interest in local history, I trust that this may be regarded as some qualification for undertaking this study of an old Devonshire town, and for following its historic byways.

I take this opportunity of acknowledging my indebtedness to the authors and publishers of those works mentioned in the Bibliography, to which frequent reference has been made. In particular, I acknowledge my debt to Professor W. G. Hoskins, C.B.E., whose books on local history have been of inestimable help to me. And I am deeply grateful for the constant encouragement I have received from many friends, which spurred me on to complete this book.

My thanks are also due to Mrs. Elsie Archer, whose enthusiasm for the subject has led her to undertake the typing of the manuscript for me.

Finally, but by no means least, I wish to express my thanks to my publishers for their guidance and help; and also to my wife for her constant encouragement and support, which has so largely contributed in making this work possible.

JOHN A. WHITHAM

Ottery St Mary,
Devon.

1984

ACKNOWLEDGEMENTS

The author and publishers wish to thank the following for permission to reproduce the photographs included in this book:

Aerofilms Limited, Boreham Wood, Herts, plate 3; Ottery Church Corporation, plate 6; National Portrait Gallery, London, plates 12, 13 and 20; The Governing Body, Christ Church, Oxford, plate 14; Lady William-Powlett, Cadhay, Ottery St Mary, plate 24; J. Salmon Limited, Sevenoaks, Kent, plate 27; East Devon News Group, Honiton, Devon (Photo: Nick Sharples), plate 30.

The author would like to express his thanks to Mr. Keith A. Bowden for his photographs (plates 4, 15, 21 and 28), and for his invaluable assistance in reproducing other illustrations for this book.

Plates 7, 16, 19, 23, 25 and 26 are reproduced by Hayes Studio, Sidmouth, Devon. Plate 29 is a photograph by the late Louis Jarché.

Line drawings: Fig. 1 specially drawn by John Yonge, Exeter; Fig. 4 drawn by D. Lambeth, A.R.I.B.A.; Fig. 5 specially drawn by Mrs. Elaine Dixon from a sketch on an old letter; and Fig. 9 from an original letter kindly lent by the late Lady Betty Cave.

The Tailpiece of the Weathercock (drawn by A. Needham) is reproduced by permission of *The Countryman*, Burford, Oxon.

The Street Plan of Ottery St Mary is drawn by John Yonge, Exeter.

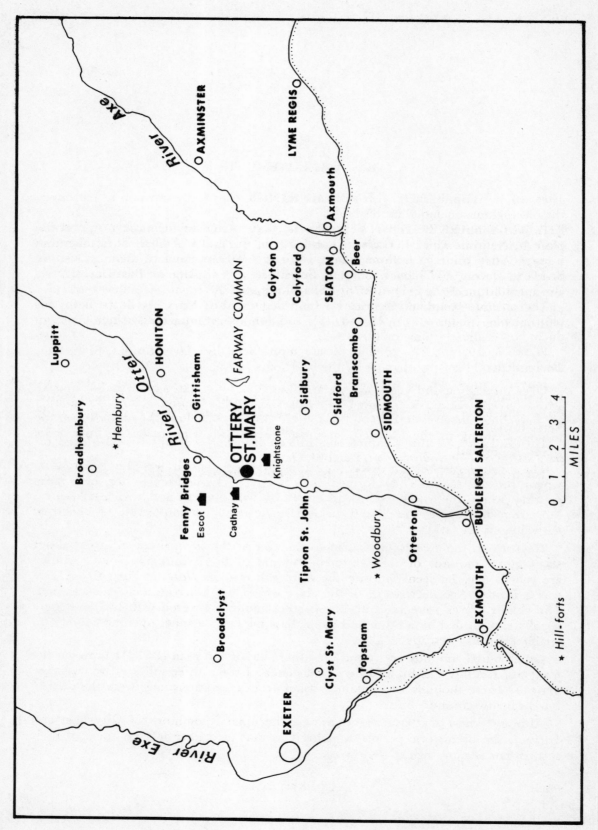

Fig. 1 Ottery St Mary and the surrounding district (*drawn by J. Yonge*)

Chapter One

BEGINNINGS

THE BUSY MARKET TOWN of Ottery St Mary stands on the eastern side of the river Otter, from which it takes its name. Set in the midst of pleasant farmlands in a green valley some 12 miles east of the city of Exeter, it is one of the most historic towns in Devon, dating back to Saxon times. From its position on the rising hillside, the splendid medieval church of St Mary dominates the town like an ever watchful and protective guardian. But no portrait of Ottery St Mary would be complete without some mention of the Bronze Age beginnings in this part of Devon.

Early settlers

Over three thousand years ago the area was thinly populated by primitive people, whose green trackways followed the ridges of the surrounding hills. Frequently we may find ourselves today following some grassy track along the hills, or over the moors, treading in the footsteps of those early tribes, who made the first green roads of England.

The Bronze Age settlers were the earliest farmers, and it was their civilisation which set the scene. They formed their scattered farmsteads in the high open country where there was less risk of attack by wild animals and hostile tribesmen. Moreover, the dense woods and marshes made it almost impossible to penetrate the valley of the Otter.

High up on the greensand plateau to the east of the town there still exist about sixty burial mounds of these farmers. Several of these 'round barrows', as they are called, may be seen opposite the *Hare and Hounds Hotel* at Putts Cross. This was a Bronze Age necropolis, or the place where a number of ancient tracks met. The simple graves were built up into earthen mounds covered with turf, and were usually surrounded by a ditch and bank. In some cases a small opening was left to enable the soul to escape!

Other burial mounds are found on either side of the road (B3171) between the *Hare and Hounds* and Broad Down, a distance of some three miles as we cross the plateau. These mounds all contained ashes from cremations, and were the earliest burials below ground.

Although these scattered graves are on the upland commons of Gittisham and Farway, the prehistoric people who lived in that area have left no trace of their settlements nor any sign of their work.

1

Hill-forts

About five miles to the north of Ottery St Mary the ancient earthwork of Hembury Fort commands extensive views over the Otter valley, and may be seen from many parts of the town. It has been described as the grandest earthwork in Devon. Occupying the front or southern tip of a spur of the Blackdown Hills, it was originally a Neolithic[1] 'causewayed camp', but with the coming of the Bronze Age (1900–450 B.C.), it was abandoned, and remained unoccupied for over a thousand years.

During the third-century B.C. successive tribal waves of Celts came across the English Channel from Brittany in search of new territory. Many of them settled in small groups in what we know now as Devon, Cornwall, and West Somerset, and were mostly arable farmers, although some were traders. They grouped themselves together as 'the Dumnonii tribe', or 'the people of the deep land'. This tribal name was possibly taken by these people because of settling deep in the South-West, which became the Celtic Kingdom of Dumnonia.

The abandoned Neolithic camp of Hembury was chosen as their tribal centre, and it was considerably enlarged and strengthened. Now covered deep in bracken during the summer months, this ancient earthwork is 7½ acres in extent. The south slope, which rises steeply above the road between Honiton and Cullompton (A373), provided a natural defence, but on the north, where the spur joins the main ridge of the Blackdown Hills, the 'camp' was vulnerable to attack, so high protective ramparts were necessary on that side.

Excavations between 1930 and 1935 disclosed the remains of a substantial hut-site from the earlier Neolithic occupation, and traces of round querns used for grinding corn have also been found during recent years.

The Celtic tribes were largely responsible for the construction of other hill-forts in East Devon during the first-century B.C. Woodbury Castle, to the south-west of Ottery St Mary, dominates the estuary of the river Exe, whilst the pear-shaped Sidbury Castle, 1,400ft. in length, and surrounded by a double-ditch, stands high above the Sid Valley. Blackbury Castle, near Southleigh, has a single rampart, being what is known as a univallate hill-fort,[2] and Membury Castle overlooks the river Axe. North-east of Honiton is Dumpton Hill Camp, a fine hill-spur fort, with its conspicuous clump of trees.

Further evidence of Iron Age occupation (500 B.C.–A.D. 43) is found at West Hill, a mile to the west of Ottery St Mary, where the remains of Belbury Castle, 200ft. in diameter, overlook the Otter valley. The hill upon which this earthwork stands was once open heath, and was surrounded by a great ditch, part of which now forms the road on the west side. It is to be regretted that the earthen ramparts which encircled this hill-fort were obliterated about 1795. The name Belbury means 'the beautiful fort', referring to its position.

Most of these fortified hill-settlements are shown on the Ordnance Survey maps as 'Castles', and, although never such in the strict sense, they were of an individual defensive character rather than part of a general strategic scheme. The plan, construction, and size varied, but their purpose was to provide a stronghold for the protection of their immediate communities.

When the Romans came

By A.D. 49 the Romans had entered the South-West, and a powerful force was stationed near the mouth of the river Axe. This was the Second Legion under the command of Flavius Vespasian, who later became Emperor of Rome.

A great military road, known as the Fosse Way, was constructed from Axmouth to Lincoln, running diagonally across the country. A link-road joined this with Exeter (Isca Dumnoniorum),[3] and the present A30 to the north of Ottery St Mary, largely follows the line of that spear-straight Roman road. But the Romans showed little interest in the South-West beyond making Exeter their frontier.

Traces of a Roman villa have been found near Seaton, and in recent times another villa (including a Roman bath-house) has been uncovered on a farm at Holcombe, north of Lyme Regis. Cutlery, jewellery, tools, and coins were found here, and, among other treasures, a Celtic decorated bronze mirror was discovered, and is now in the British Museum.

The Roman occupation lasted for 350 years, but their great civilisation soon faded away when they departed from our shores. The South-West was left thinly peopled, and in parts abandoned. Exeter was largely deserted, with its buildings left in sad decay.

There followed a strange 'grey period' of which little is known, but the withdrawal of Roman domination created a power vacuum into which new invaders were eventually attracted in search of territorial gains. It was under these circumstances that the Saxons invaded East Devon about the year A.D. 614.

Chapter Two

THE SAXON SETTLEMENT (650–1066)

Coming of the Saxons

SAXON INVADERS landed along the Hampshire coast, coming into the river estuaries and creeks, and many of them moved northwards into Wiltshire. After making some penetration into Dorset from the north, they came onwards towards East Devon.

If we consider the geographical position of East Devon, it will be seen that to the north lay the Forest of Exmoor, the Blackdown Hills, and the extensive old Forest of Neroche, which separated Devon from Somerset. Any attempt at invasion from this direction would have been extremely difficult. But to the east there was no natural barrier separating Devon from Dorset, and so the main Saxon invasion came from this side.

The Saxons encountered some early resistance, but the native British were defeated in a fierce battle at Beandun (Bindon), near Axmouth, and over 2,000 men were killed. The fertile valleys of the rivers Axe and Coly were soon taken, and the Saxon invaders then pushed forward to the greensand plateau on the top of East Hill, overlooking the densely-wooded valley of the Otter. As this provided a natural frontier, they were content to remain here for the next 40 years before striking further west. The Otter valley and most of East Devon was then soon overrun, and, after a decisive battle near Exeter in 658, the Saxons gained control of 'the red lands' of the Exe and Culm valleys.

Three years later, a battle at Posbury, a hill-fort near Crediton, placed most of Devon in Saxon hands. The defeated British tribes took to the wooded hills in flight, and, although many were driven into Cornwall, where the Celtic influence has survived to this day, they were never completely driven out.

Settlements in the valleys

The Saxon invaders, weary of war and conquest, went in search of new lands to cultivate and farm, for they were essentially country dwellers. The prehistoric peoples had made their primitive settlements on the high ground, largely for defensive purposes, but the Saxons sought the shelter of the valleys for their farmsteads, and carved out clearings in the forests where they could settle with their families and followers.

4

The story of Ottery (*Otrei*) really begins with the coming of the Saxons. They tended to settle in small compact communities under their particular leader, or chief, and the early settlements, which were built near fresh water, consisted of a group of buildings, so forming a village or hamlet. Many of the fields extending up the lower slopes of the hills in this part of Devon were originally hacked out of the dense natural woodlands far back in Saxon times.

The Saxon settlers built their farmsteads with the timber at hand and surrounded them with a stockade of wooden posts for protection. Attached to each farmstead were open fields which were tilled in common, the heavy task of clearing the forests and undergrowth or draining the marshlands being shared.

The Saxon tun (or -ton)

The Saxon chief gave his name to the cluster of farmsteads where he and his people dwelt, and this became known as his tun (or later, -ton), from which the word 'town' is derived. The original meaning of tun was 'an area enclosed by a fence', but in course of time it came to refer to the actual settlement itself. For example, Alfington, near Ottery St Mary, was the farmstead of a Saxon leader called Aelfa and his family. Wiggaton was 'the settlement of Wicga and his followers', and Tipton (St John was added much later) was Tippa's farmstead or settlement.

There are some 170 place-names in Devon formed before the Norman Conquest which terminate in -ton, and have the personal name of some early settler as their first element. The earliest names which have survived are those of our rivers, for most river-names are of Celtic origin, although in many cases the meaning has been lost in the mists of time. The river Otter may have been so named long before Saxon times because of the otters which inhabited its banks. The Anglo-Saxon (or Old English) word meaning an otter was very similar, being ōter. Ēa meant 'a water or stream' in the sense of denoting a river, and, if this is added as a suffix, we have ōterēa or 'Otter river'.

The Anglo-Saxon farmsteads or settlements were in many cases named after the rivers or streams upon or near whose banks they stood. In his *Survey of the County of Devon,* published in 1714, Tristram Risdon quaintly described Ottery St Mary as 'the prime place to which the River Otter communicateth its name'.

The 'radial pattern' of Saxon settlements

The early Saxon settlers tended to follow the plan of the Celts, who, long before the Roman occupation of Britain, built their dwellings where a number of tracks and lanes met. So, too, the Saxons chose as the sites for their settlements 'the meeting of the ways'—a central hub, or nucleus, with tracks leading into it from all directions.

The dwellings were built around the fringe of a rectangular open space for defensive purposes. From this we get the origin of 'the village green'. At night the livestock was brought within the enclosure for protection. This 'star-shaped' settlement is characteristic of Saxon origin, and is well illustrated by Ottery St

Mary. It may also be traced at Sidbury (where seven lanes converge), whilst other good examples of Saxon nucleated settlements in East Devon are found at Broadhembury, Colyton and Woodbury.

'Sunken-lane' boundaries

The study of Saxon boundaries is of considerable interest, for they were the earliest field-boundaries in the country.

So as to make clear divisions between the large Saxon estates, the powerful landowners used slave labour to dig wide ditches along their boundaries. The earth from these was thrown up in high mounds, so as to form a continuous bank on either side. In this way, a 'double-ditch' was formed, which became a sunken lane, enclosed between high earthen banks. On the top of these banks, trees and hedges were planted, so creating what was called 'a hollow way'. As these lanes merely extended for the length of the estate boundary, they frequently end rather abruptly.

It will be seen from what has been said, that the narrow Devon lanes, so well known to us, were in many cases the estate boundaries of Saxon times.

The shire

The division of the Anglo-Saxon kingdoms into shires (so called from O.E. *scyran*, meaning 'to divide') is ascribed to King Alfred and, although he may have introduced the system into England, it had been established among the Franks in the sixth century.

The Saxon invaders of Devon applied the Celtic tribal name of Dumnonii to the shire, their version being 'Defnas'. The inhabitants became known as 'the Defenum', and as the Celtic 'f' was pronounced as 'v', the shire of Devon retained its British name.

The earliest reference to Devonshire appears in an Anglo-Saxon Charter dated 851, but it had possibly become a shire before this. The system of territorial division was created in order to encourage better government and easier administration of justice. The chief officer was the shire-reeve (later known as the Sheriff), who was appointed by the Crown every year.

The hundred

Late in Saxon times the shires were divided into districts called hundreds, 'for the adjustment of taxation, the maintenance of peace and order and the settlement of local pleas'.[1]

There were originally 36 of these sub-divisions in Devon. In theory, the hundred comprised an area of 100 hides, but it varied greatly as to extent in different parts of England. As determined by local usage, a hide could be 60, 80, 100, or even 120 acres. It was such an area as might be ploughed with a single ox-plough, or as much as would maintain a family.

Ottery was a hundred in itself, being divided into two almost equal parts by the river Otter. It was co-extensive with the parish, and was so shown on the Geld Roll.[2]

Each hundred had its own court and was governed by a high constable or bailiff. The men of the hundred were called 'the Hundredors'.

The tithing

Each hundred was sub-divided into tithings (the name still survives in Somerset and Wiltshire) and in these small areas lived 10 freeholders with their families, who were knit together in a society. They were bound to the king for their peaceable and good behaviour, and the tithing-man, who was the chief among them, was appointed annually. Together these 10 men made up the frankpledge which was a system of preserving the peace by forming groups of 10 freeholders and making each member a surety for the good behaviour of the others, including their families.

The Danes

Some Viking raids took place towards the end of the Anglo-Saxon period. Exeter was their main objective and in 1001, following a fierce attack which was repelled, the Danish invaders wreaked their vengeance on East Devon, plundering and burning down the villages of Pinhoe and Broadclyst 'and also many goodly towns that we cannot name'. Names such as 'Danes Wood', to the north-west of Broadclyst, and 'Danes Mill' in Plymtree parish are a reminder of their presence in these parts.

Two years later (1003) Exeter was betrayed to the Danes, who burnt down and plundered the whole city. Shortly afterwards Devon was to pass with the rest of Wessex into Danish rule under King Cnut (1017–1035). Exeter, like the phoenix rose again from its ashes and made a marvellous recovery to become the most important town in Devon. By this time, the old Celtic tribe of Dumnonii had withdrawn to the west of Cornwall, in that extreme toe known as the Penrith peninsula.

Edward the Confessor (1042–1066)

In 1042 Edward the Confessor unexpectedly became king, and the Anglo-Saxon line was restored after the interlude of Danish rule. Edward was Norman by birth and had been brought up a prince with no thought of a throne. His long years of exile in Normandy had been spent in the company of Norman and French ecclesiastics, and, much influenced by religious life, he came to devote himself to works of piety. He was not a great scholar and, in fact, during his years in exile he had spent much of his time in hunting and idleness, which tastes remained with him all his life. He appointed his Norman favourites to the high places of Church and State, and, as he was childless, he wished his great-nephew, William, Duke of Normandy, to succeed him.

Edward the Confessor was at heart more French than English, and he may be said to have paved the way for the Norman Conquest in 1066. These strong Norman sympathies were to have a considerable bearing on the future history of Ottery.

The earliest document in which Ottery (*Otrei*) is mentioned is a Saxon Charter dated 1061 whereby the bounds of the manor and parish were fixed.[3] It was about this time that the town mill was built astride the mill stream or leat.

In 1061 Edward the Confessor decided to grant the manor of Ottery ('*quandam villam nomine Otregiam*') to the canons of the cathedral church of St Mary at Rouen in Normandy. He declared that he did so 'for the salvation and redemption of his Soul and in order that the Virgin might intercede for his sins with Our Lord Jesus Christ'. Ottery was to remain a possession of the canons of Rouen for the next 275 years.

Beating the parish bounds

In the chapter library at Canterbury is preserved a copy of the Anglo-Saxon Charter of 1061, which carefully recorded the landmarks along the bounds of the manor of Ottery. This copy of the Charter was made in 1227, but the Norman transcription of the Saxon letters, due to ignorance of that alphabet, has made identification of the names of the boundary landmarks difficult. They are, however, of considerable interest and an attempt will be made here to follow them in clockwise direction.[4]

The manor created the parish and the boundaries were normally co-extensive. We start at Straightway Head at the north-west corner of the parish. This was *straet geate*—the gate or gap where the former Roman road (O.E. *straet*) from Honiton to Exeter came through a depression in the hills. Straitgate Farm nearby preserves the Anglo-Saxon name. From here we move eastwards to *taelenford* (Taleford) 'the crossing over the River Tale'. The river-name Tale is of Celtic derivation and means 'the swift stream'.

The little river is followed upstream as far as *blindan pylle* ('the blind stream'). At this point the boundary turns sharply eastwards to *dene beorg,* the barrow or early burial mound in the valley. This tumulus was near the present railway line and was removed over 100 years ago, but has given its name to fields called Denbury. We continue onwards to *haeo feld mere* meaning 'open land on the boundary covered with heather', from which a nearby field is still named Heathfield Brank.

We come to the river Otter at *straet pol,* which meant 'the deep place in the river by the Roman road', and is better known to us today as Fenny Bridges. There was possibly a ford (*straetford*) at this point where the old Roman road (now the busy A30) crossed the river Otter before a bridge was built. A small stream called the Vine (*finan*) joins the Otter here as a tributary.

After crossing the river, the boundary leads away along a track known as Gittisham Landscore, which separates the parishes of Ottery and Gittisham and makes in the direction of East Hill.

A Saxon estate boundary or 'hollow way' is followed to the 'red flood' (*Raedan flodan*), the red intermittent spring, so named because of the reddish water produced from the sandstone stratum. Continuing on Westgate Hill (*Bromdune midward*) and along the old ridgeway, across the top of Chineway and forward under the crest of East Hill, we join the boundary of the estate called *Wigincland*.[5] Below us in the valley on our right is Wiggaton, the tūn or farmstead of Wicga, possibly associated with *Wigincland*. The manor of Ottery comprised two separate estates of almost equal size. One of these was *Wigincland* and the other was called *Otriglands,* but the line of the boundary between them, which ran diagonally across the manor, cannot now be identified with any accuracy.

Continuing southwards along the ridgeway, the boundary leads above Waxway (*Waecc's Way*) to Wacca's tree (*Waecc's treow*), near what is now known as White Cross (*Whiteburrow*). On our way towards this point, we pass on the right open picnic areas with extensive views westwards across the Otter valley to the distant heights of Dartmoor.

Although the road swings to the left at White Cross, and drops down to Sidbury, we continue ahead along the ridge track to Hollow Head Cross—*berrdes cumbes heafod*[6]—at the upper end of Burscombe, a deep valley running down to Sidford between the Iron Age hill-fort of Sidbury Castle and the spur of Core Hill. This eastern side of East Hill is, in fact, broken by several deep coombs which have cut themselves into the soft marl.

It is a short step to Beacon Hill (*Leofan dune*). Identification of the Anglo-Saxon landmarks becomes increasingly difficult as we drop down into the valley, attempting to follow the parish boundary across the river Otter, and make our way in the direction of Metcombe. Points of demarcation often consisted of particular trees, prominent stones or springs which have long since disappeared.

Below us is Harpford Wood (O.E. *cetes holt*), which was formerly called Chettisholt (1612), and making for this we pass through to reach the river Otter at *borstenan clife*—'a broken cliff'. Then, turning southwards, we cross by a ford. The ancient trackway leading up out of the valley past Metcombe towards Aylesbeare Common is followed until the boundary turns northwards where, after passing the site of an apple tree, it crosses the West Brook by a ford (Stoneford).

We continue on to reach the ancient ridge-track (reputed to have been a Roman road, but possibly older) at what is now called Tipton Cross.[7] This was probably neutral territory where the three parishes joined.

Having reached this ridge-road, which forms the boundary between Ottery and Rockbeare, we go northwards to *straetgeat* (Straightway Head) where our journey began.

In the Middle Ages it was the duty of the parish officials to walk round or perambulate the parish annually, usually during Rogationtide when the crops were blessed, to reaffirm the extent of the parish.[8] On their circuitous journey they were accompanied by local boys, who were bumped or bounced on boundary stones, beaten, whipped, ducked in ponds, and even stood on their heads at certain ancient landmarks, so as to impress them on their young minds and that they, in turn, would be able to pass on this knowledge to future generations.

This ancient custom of 'beating the bounds', as it was called, is still observed in many parishes, although parish boundaries have been fixed by Act of Parliament, and the more general use of maps has rendered this no longer necessary. It became the ritual to beat the landmarks with long canes with the same object of impressing the places on the boys' memories, but in a less painful manner!

Curses were often placed upon any person who moved or altered the position of a boundary mark, and even today there are certain old stones which are known to have a curse attached to them. But the bounds of a parish were of considerable importance and had to be remembered in order to prevent encroachment and to deal with disputes.

Coming of Christianity

A word must be said about the coming of Christianity. Although a number of Celtic missionary saints had landed on the coasts of Cornwall, Christianity was slow to arrive in Devon, particularly in East Devon, which had been under Roman occupation.

When St Augustine landed in Britain in the year 597 and became first Archbishop of Canterbury, Celtic missionaries in the South-West had already introduced the faith. By early Saxon times the influence of Celtic Christianity had made itself felt in this part of Devon, and the work of conversion proceeded gradually. It should be remembered that the Saxons reached Devon somewhat later than other parts of Britain and were by then mostly Christians.

A small monastery was founded at Exeter during the seventh century and dedicated to St Mary and St Peter. This possibly emanated from the great abbey at Glastonbury. We learn that about the year 690 Winfrith, who was born at Crediton and later became St Boniface, was, when a boy, placed in the care of the abbot at Exeter.

In 909 the diocese of Crediton was formed comprising the whole of Devon, and by 1050 this became the diocese of Exeter, which covered Cornwall and Devon. Both these counties had originally been included in the large see of Sherborne, which was created as far back as the year 705.

A new Benedictine abbey was built at Exeter in 932, but when the city was sacked by the Danes at the beginning of the next century, the Saxon abbey was plundered and destroyed by fire. It was King Cnut who rebuilt the minster in 1018 and it had a widespread Christian influence upon the area during the next 100 years.

In 1050, King Edward the Confessor, accompanied by his queen, enthroned Leofric as first bishop of Exeter, and the small Saxon minster became a cathedral.

Meanwhile, many early churches, called 'minsters', were founded in Devon and over four hundred of these have survived to the present day. Besides Exeter abbey there was Tavistock abbey, which was founded about 974, and Buckfast abbey, founded in 1018. Axminster was one of the earliest Saxon settlements in Devon and took its name from the minster, or *monasterium,* by the river Axe, being founded by Athelstan, King of Wessex (925–39). Similarly, Exminster was named after the early Saxon monastery by the Exe.

By the time of the Norman Conquest, Devon had been converted to the Christian faith, and much of the county had been under Anglo-Saxon rule for over three hundred years.

Chapter Three

THE EARLY MIDDLE AGES (1066–1307)

THE MANOR OF OTREI is shown in Domesday Book (1086)[1] as being held of William the Conqueror by the Chapter of the Cathedral Church of St Mary at Rouen, and that it was let to farm at a rental of 66 marks.[2] It is stated that there were eight hides (about 800 acres) of pasture, 100 acres of meadow land and 20 acres of forest or woodland. Of this land, the Canons of Rouen were in occupation of some 500 acres. The revenue appears to have been derived mainly from pig-keepers and millers.

The Domesday entry records that there were 24 husbandmen or cottagers (*bordarii*), each with a small piece of land allowed to them in return for produce; 55 villeins or servile tenants (*villani*), who were by birth and inheritance bound to the soil for life and confined to the precincts of the manor; 17 labourers (*servi*) and five swineherds. It is also mentioned that there was a garden and a saltwork at Sidmouth (*Sedemude*), which was then an appendage of the Church of St Michael's Mount in Normandy. (*See* Appendix A.)

Of the 98 water-mills in Devon, three are recorded as being in the manor of Otrei, and the name Mill Street indicates the place to which it led. These mills belonged to the lord of the manor, who could insist that his servile tenants brought their corn to be ground there at his price. It is possible that the millers of the South-West preferred to continue using the ancient method of the hand-quern, which would account for the low number of mills in this part of the country. According to the Domesday Survey there were about six thousand water-mills in England at that time, and of the small number in Devon, most of these were in the south-east corner of the county, being on the rivers Exe, Axe and Otter. But it was not until the reign of Edward I (1272–1307) that the fulling-mill (also known as a tucking-mill) for stamping cloth by water-driven hammers, made its appearance in East Devon, and the weaving of fine broadcloth was soon taking place there.

Early vicars

Although Domesday Book makes no mention of a church or other religious building (*aeccle*) at Ottery, there could have been a small Saxon church. In his *General Introduction to Domesday*, Ellis says, 'It should however, be observed that the Commissioners were not instructed to make a return of Churches, so that the mention of them, if made at all, was likely to be irregular'. It must be borne in mind that Domesday Book was essentially a tax book and was prepared with that end in view.

After the Norman Conquest little was done to repair or restore churches until the beginning of the 12th century, when the wealthy Norman landowners set about building and reconstructing churches of every size and type throughout the country. Patrons, ecclesiastics, and, at a later date, the religious guilds formed by zealous parishioners, were often responsible for the foundation, rebuilding or enlargement of parish churches.

We know from the old registers of the cathedral church of St Mary at Rouen that in the reign of Henry II (1154–1189) William and Roger were vicars of Ottery. Furthermore, it is recorded that in 1191 Peter the Clerk resigned and was succeeded by Roger the Chaplain, which indicates the existence of a church at that time.

The fuller name of Ottery St Mary appears to have originated early in the 13th century, for there is a reference to 'Sca. Maria de Otery' in 1207, and to 'Sce Marie Otery' in 1238. 'St Mary' became an adjunct to the place-name when the church was dedicated. The Book of Fees in 1242 shows it as 'Otery Sancte Marie'.

The earliest mention of a church here is found in the Register of Walter Bronescombe, Bishop of Exeter (1257–1280), where it is shown that he set out from his palace at Crediton on tours of his diocese dedicating various churches. In the week commencing 3 December 1259 this energetic bishop, whose tomb in Exeter Cathedral displays unsurpassed craftsmanship, proceeded on such a tour, visiting Broadhembury, Ottery St Mary, Dunkeswell, Sheldon, Kentisbeare, and Sampford Peverell. The entry which is in Latin, records that:

> In this year [1259] on Jupiter's Day after the Feast of St Andrew [Thursday 4 December] Bishop Bronescombe dedicated the Church of Sancte Marie de Otery.

This was possibly the dedication of some addition to the original church, such as a new altar or chapel.

Markets and fairs

The great age of fairs began in medieval times and it became of increasing importance to acquire legal status for these fairs by obtaining a charter. In some cases they were granted in recognition of services rendered to the king.

The distinction between a fair and a market was that a fair was open to everyone on specific days in each year, whereas at a market the selling was limited to those people who enjoyed the benefit of local privileges.

In 1226 Henry III granted a Charter to the Dean and Chapter of St Mary's cathedral church at Rouen conferring the right to hold a market and fair at Ottery St Mary. The granting of charters to religious houses enabled them to derive the benefit of all tolls, fees and duties, and assured them of a considerable income.

The Flexton was the site of the open market-place of Ottery St Mary, and it was here, at the top of Church Hill (now Silver Street), that the great fairs and markets were held. This was the busy centre of the secular life of the town, and the Flexton was the chief trading area.

'. . . with lighted candles and sounded bells'

During the 13th century the Church was to pass through some turbulent times. In the year 1275 information was received by Bishop Bronescombe that 'some persons, satellites of Satan, desiring to break down the strength of ecclesiastical discipline and to lay their hands on that which was not lawful', were planning 'with great violence and an armed band' to rob William of St Gorone, the vicar of Ottery church, of 'the fruits and rights belonging to it'. Whereupon the bishop commanded the archdeacon of Exeter in order 'to frustrate the iniquitous plan' to call together the priests of the Deanery of Aylesbeare and other neighbouring clergy and send them 'clothed in their priestly robes and walking in procession' to the church, so as to dissuade the violators from their evil intention under pain of greater excommunication. If they persisted in their wickedness then it should be declared 'publicly and solemnly with lighted candles and sounded bells' that such sentence had been imposed upon them, and their names should be obtained and reported to the bishop.

Less than two months later the bishop issued a precept to the archdeacon commanding that William, the Abbot of Forde, near Chard, should appear before him in the cathedral 'to answer for the violation of a sequestration of the fruits of the Church of St Mary, Ottery and for divers other excesses'.

In what was mainly a self-contained agricultural community, men and women tilled the land and worked hard to make sufficient money to meet the demands of their rapacious overlords. They lived and died in the place of their birth, for they were never able to move far from it.

But eventually the oppressive influence and the severe extortions of the Dean and Chapter of Rouen brought growing resentment to a head. In July 1283, the manor of Ottery was let to Walter de Lechelade, Precentor of Exeter Cathedral, for his life, and although the lease was recognised and approved by Bishop Peter Quivil (1280–1291), it appears to have been contrary to the Canons of the Council of London, 1236. The more money the precentor could extort from the unfortunate inhabitants of Ottery, the more would be available for him after accounting for the rent to the Canons of Rouen.

Bitter resentment was soon to be expressed in violence, for only four months later, on 9 November 1283, the precentor was murdered by 'certain sons of perdition, full of fiendish ferocity' in the cathedral yard at Exeter. The mayor and the porter of the south gate were both hanged for having allowed the gate to be open at night! Twenty-one persons appear to have been involved in this outrage within the precincts of the cathedral, of whom 11 were clergy.

Among those implicated was John de Wolfrington, vicar of Ottery St Mary, who, after three years' detention in the bishop's prison, successfully claimed 'Benefit of Clergy' and obtained his release. This and similar unhappy incidents give some indication of the state of unrest that prevailed in this little community at that time.

On the night of the feast of St Gregory the Pope (12 March 1286) an attempt was made by a man named Richard de la Hulle and others to rob the granary at Ottery St Mary belonging to the Dean and Chapter of Rouen. The dean's servant, Philip Bateman, resisted the attempt and struck the leader with such force that he died in prison the following day. An Inquisition was held at Honiton on

11 June 1286 to enquire into the circumstances leading to de la Hulle's death, and a full account of the affair was given.

John de Grandisson becomes Bishop of Exeter

Among the early vicars of Ottery the name of John de Middleton appears in 1297. Then came Gulfridus, who died in 1310, and the living was conferred on John de Thormerton on condition that he resided in the parish. Next we come across John de Sharnebok, who was instituted on 17 October 1329 contrary to the rights of the patrons to appoint, so this was revoked by Letters Patent under the Royal Seal on 22 January 1331, and full power was given to recover possession of the church. (*See* Appendix C.)

Meanwhile, in the year 1326, there had occurred something which was to lead to a great change in the fortunes and history of the town. Walter de Stapeldon, Bishop of Exeter (1308–26) was murdered by the mob in London. He was Lord Treasurer to the unpopular Edward II, and, because of his friendship with the king, he was set upon by an incensed mob and killed. His body was brought back to Exeter and his tomb has a place of honour on the north side of the high altar in the cathedral.

He was succeeded as bishop by James de Berkeley, whose premature death brought his episcopate to a sudden end after only 14 weeks. The see of Exeter was vacant for a second time in less than a year.

Our attention now turns across the English Channel. The Papal Court was at Avignon in France when the news came of Bishop Berkeley's death. The chaplain to Pope John XXII was a certain John de Grandisson. The Pope's choice fell upon him and he was appointed to the vacant see of Exeter. His consecration as the new bishop took place on Sunday, 18 October 1327, in the Dominican Church at Avignon, and after paying homage to Edward III at York, he was enthroned in Exeter Cathedral on the octave of the Assumption (22 August 1328) as the 17th bishop.

Chapter Four

THE COLLEGIATE FOUNDATION (1337–1545)

JOHN DE GRANDISSON was born at Ashperton, near Hereford, in 1292. His father, William, Lord de Grandisson, was a member of a noble Burgundian family and had come to England attached to the household of Edmund, Earl of Lancaster, brother of Edward I. Lord de Grandisson had, as a baron of the realm, been summoned to parliament from 1299 to 1325. On the death of his first wife, by whom he had two sons, he married Sybilla, daughter and co-heiress of John, Lord Tregoz, of Castle Ewias in Herefordshire. She was the granddaughter of Juliana, sister of St Thomas de Cantilupe, Bishop of Hereford (1275–82).

Lord de Grandisson and his wife, Sybilla, had five sons (three of whom took Holy Orders) and four daughters. John de Grandisson was their second son.

After studying theology at the University of Paris, he was made a Prebendary of Masham in York Minster (1309–15) at the early age of seventeen. Nine years later he became Archdeacon of Nottingham, and on the death of his younger brother, Thomas, succeeded him in Heydore Prebend at Lincoln Cathedral in 1318. He was also a Canon and Prebendary of Wells Cathedral. As chaplain to Pope John XXII, he was serving on a Commission to negotiate the peace of Gascony, when news of the sudden death of James de Berkeley reached the Papal Court.

Shortly after his enthronement as Bishop of Exeter at the age of 35, John de Grandisson dedicated the high altar in the cathedral,[1] and so' completed the work of his three predecessors, Bishops Quivil, Bitton and Stapledon.[2] The rebuilding and enlargement of the Norman cathedral had been begun about the year 1272 by Bishop Bronescombe and this great work progressed over the next 80 years. John de Grandisson, shortly after becoming bishop, wrote to Pope John XXII: '. . . the Cathedral of Exeter, now finished up to the Nave, is marvellous in beauty and when completed will surpass every Gothic Church in England and Wales'.

But whilst this building work was progressing, Grandisson was turning his attention to another direction. He had a long-formed wish to found an establishment which might be a sanctuary for piety and learning. The situation that he judged most

Fig. 2

**Arms of John de Grandisson,
Bishop of Exeter
(1327–69)**

Paly of six argent and azure, a bend gules charged with a mitre argent between two eagles or

15

suitable for the purpose was Ottery; the position was pleasant, fertile and salubrious. It was within easy reach of Exeter, so he could, without prejudice to his episcopal obligations, watch its foundation and attend to its rising growth. Moreover, his successors in the see of Exeter would be able by their presence to give proper supervision and keep alive the spirit of fervour and religious discipline.

And so, by the year 1334, with the approbation of his sovereign, Edward III, and his patron, Pope John XXII,[3] Bishop Grandisson was writing to the Archbishop of Rouen: 'There is a certain Estate or Manor in our Diocese of Exeter with its Parish Church annexed which could serve no Divine or human purpose better than by becoming an everlasting possession to us and our successors and the Cathedral of Exeter'.

But the negotiations for the purchase of the manor of Ottery and its church were to prove difficult, for the Chapter of Rouen seems to have been intent on driving a hard bargain. The demands of the canons were so high that we find Bishop Grandisson describing them as being unreasonable and exorbitant—'summa gravis et intolerabilis et salva gratia vestra irrationabilis'.

The letters which passed between the parties during these negotiations are preserved in Bishop Grandisson's Register. 'You seem to demand', he wrote, 'a heavy, excessive, intolerable and, with all due respect, a ridiculous sum which it is unlikely that anybody would pay or offer for all you possess in our Diocese, which hardly pays you 140 marks a year.'

Eventually, Bishop Grandisson was successful, although he considered the price was still too high. The deed of conveyance was sealed on 13 June 1335, and the entire cost of purchasing the manor and church of Ottery was borne by the bishop out of his own purse, 'ex suo peculio', but the actual figure is not mentioned. As soon as the sale was completed, the canons of Rouen were ready to admit that, owing to the distance, and dangers of war, the possession had long ceased to be of much value to them!

The royal licence for the founding of the college at Ottery St Mary was granted by Edward III on 15 December 1337, and on Christmas Eve Bishop Grandisson presented the church to the warden and canons of his new foundation. The college consisted of 40 members. The principal dignitaries in residence were the warden (who was the head of the college); then the minister; the chanter (or precentor) and the sacrist. They were to have the rank of canons and prebendaries. In addition were four other canons, who were at least sub-deans, making eight canons in all.

Further members of the collegiate foundation consisted of: eight choral vicars in priests' orders; a parish priest; a morn priest, whose duty it was to celebrate the early morning service (he resided at the gatehouse, which later came to be called 'Mornt House', at the south entrance to the churchyard) and Our Lady's chaplain, who was attached to the Lady Chapel and was also songmaster for the choirboys; eight clerks, or secondaries; two church clerks (clerici Ecclesie); two holy-water clerks (clericis aquebaulis);[4] eight chorister boys; and a master of grammar.

All these members of the college were required to assist at the daily and nightly office in the church. The parish priest and the two holy-water clerks were to be appointed by the minister, whilst the two church clerks were appointed by the sacrist, and the other members were appointed by the resident canons.

The government of the college was prescribed by the 'Ordinacio Primaria', which was dated 22 January 1338. This was followed by the Statutes on 29 September 1339.

Meanwhile the fabric of the former parish church was being moulded and transformed into a magnificent collegiate church which, with its liturgical arrangements, was modelled with much care upon Bishop Grandisson's cathedral at Exeter. The transepts of the original church were unroofed and raised as massive twin towers. The nave and chancel were enlarged, and square vestries were added on either side. The crowning glory of Grandisson's collegiate church was the lady chapel, approached under an elegant stone minstrels' gallery. The church was rich with colour and included the heraldic arms of Bishop Grandisson and members of his illustrious family. Those of the bishop, and of Monta-cute, alternate on either side throughout the entire length of the main vaulting. The great work of rebuilding was com-pleted about the year 1342.

By his magnanimous action, John de Grandisson had not only released the people of Ottery from the bondage of Rouen, but the town now stood on the threshold of a glorious era in its history, which was to last for over two hundred years. Ottery's place on the map had been estab-lished for all time.

Although Bishop Grandisson had done much to benefit the people of Ottery St Mary by choosing their town for his splendid collegiate church, they showed him little gratitude. His new tenants were to cause him trouble from the start. They complained about him to the Earl of Devon, who in turn placed these grievances before Grandisson himself. He was incensed by such behaviour, and on 30 August 1335 sent a stinging rejoinder reproving his noble

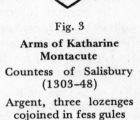

Fig. 3

Arms of Katharine Montacute
Countess of Salisbury (1303–48)

Argent, three lozenges cojoined in fess gules

'Cousin Courtenay' for his interference and declared that his tenants at Ottery St Mary were guilty of malice and disobedience. The result of this was a new scheme for the running of the manor and the control of his turbulent tenants.

Of the architectural features of Bishop Grandisson's collegiate church, the twin transeptal towers are outstanding. They are 64ft. in height and that on the north is surmounted by a spire. The north tower of Exeter Cathedral had a similar spire until 1752. Apart from the cathedral, the only church in England which has transepts formed by towers is that at Ottery St Mary. Characteristic of Bishop Grandisson's work are the pointed arches of the clerestory windows.

The weathercock on the spire is believed to be the oldest still in use in this country and is known as 'the Whistling Cock' because of the noise formerly caused by the wind blowing through two tubes in the base. From the beak to the tip of the tail the bird is 2ft. 3in. and stands 15½in. high. It is of cast bronze with a brass comb.

On the cornice of the richly ornamented altar screen are displayed the shields of arms of Grandisson and members of his family. In the centre are the royal arms of France ancient, and those of England.[5] These arms were originally painted on a flat surface, and it was not until 1833 that Edward Blore (1787–1879) cut them in stone (*see* Chapter VIII).

The beautifully-canopied stone sedilia on the south side of the sanctuary is a particularly fine example, for sedilia were at their richest during the Decorated period of the 14th century.

As Bishop Grandisson had been a prebendary of Wells Cathedral it seems likely that the richly-moulded ribs of the chancel ceiling follow the similar arrangement of small quatrefoil panels at Wells, which are for ornamentation only. His brother William had succeeded him as prebendary there in 1327, and it is possible that craftsmen from Wells were sent to carry out this work at Ottery St Mary. Wells Cathedral has, of course, its ancient clock, and likewise has Exeter, so it is hardly surprising to find in Grandisson's collegiate church another of our earliest clocks. Its age must be largely a matter of conjecture, but it is generally attributed to John de Grandisson, and claims to be one of the oldest surviving mechanical clocks in the country. It was placed on a wooden gallery in what was the college bell-tower, where a clock was necessary to regulate 'the time of fast and festival, prayer and vigil, solemn chant and stately ceremonial during the centuries of time'.

The earth was regarded as the centre of the solar system, and the square wooden clock-face shows the phases of the moon as well as the hours of day and night.

The earliest reference to the existence of a clock in the church appears in the college rolls (*compotos*) for the year 1437–38, where among entries of payments for tallow, wicks and rushes, there is recorded a payment of three shillings and fourpence (17p) for the care of the clock ('Et pro Custodia Horologii 3s. 4d.').

A further entry in the Register appears during the year Michaelmas 1496–97:

> Care of the Clock 3s. 4d. per annum. Thomas Clockmaker of Exeter for himself 8d. [3p] per day for his work and allowance for his horse. First, for seeing to our Clock, with board and fodder for his horse and repairs of Clock, 10s. 4d. [52p].

Grandisson's wooden eagle lectern

There was a stone screen across the entrance to the chancel, as in Exeter Cathedral, and we are told that this was 'broad and solid'. It was about 10ft. in height and 6ft. in depth with a stone staircase leading up to the rood-loft above the screen. In the case of cathedrals and collegiate churches it was usual for the epistle and gospel to be read from the rood-loft or 'pulpitum'.

Most medieval figure lecterns took the form of an eagle, and one is shown on the Luttrell Psalter (*c.* 1340). They were made of wood and usually painted. In 1342 Bishop Grandisson gave to his collegiate church the gilded wooden eagle lectern, which was originally on the rood-loft and, when viewed from below, only the eagle would have been visible above the top of the screen. This lectern now stands in the lady chapel, and is mounted on an early Victorian carved wooden stand with the arms of Bishop Grandisson displayed on either side.

1. Seal of the College (1342-1545).

2. Seal of John de Grandisson, Bishop of Exeter (1327-69).

3. (*overleaf*) Ottery St Mary: an aerial view.

4. (*left*) John de Grandisson, Bishop of Exeter (1327-69): a corbel on the south wall of the Lady Chapel of the Collegiate Church of St Mary of Ottery.

5. (*above*) Roof boss in the chancel of the Collegiate Church: Madonna and Child. (A special Christmas postage stamp for 8p was based on this boss in 1974.)

6. (*below*) The Collegiate Church. (From a water-colour drawing, about 1840.)

7. From 'an original Drawing of the Screen at the back of the High Altar in the St Mary Ottery Church, Devon . . .' by V. Bonner, 1792.

8. Alexander Barclay (1475?-1552): poet, scholar and divine. He was chaplain to the Collegiate Church of St Mary, Ottery from 1490 until 1511.

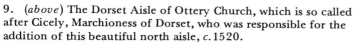

9. (*above*) The Dorset Aisle of Ottery Church, which is so called after Cicely, Marchioness of Dorset, who was responsible for the addition of this beautiful north aisle, *c.*1520.

10. (*top right*) The Ottery Elephant: pier-cap decoration (*c.*1520).

11. (*right*) Monument of John Coke (1589-1632) of Thorne, Ottery St Mary. This gloomy memorial is in the Dorset Aisle of the Church.

12. (*top left*) Sir Thomas Fairfax (1612-71). (Engraving by W. Faithorne.)

13. (*above*) Samuel Taylor Coleridge (1772-1834). (Painting by Peter Vandyke, 1795.)

14. (*left*) The Rt. Rev. William Hart Coleridge, D.D. (1789-1849), first Bishop of Barbados and the Leeward Islands. (Painting by Thomas Phillips, R.A.)

15. (*above*) The ancient stocks in Ottery churchyard.
16. (*below*) The Factory and St Saviour's Bridge, *c.*1820.

17. (*opposite above*) Cadhay Bridge over the River Otter.
18. (*opposite below*) The Tumbling Weir (*c.*1789) and the old mill-house.

19. Interior of the Church looking towards the chancel. (Drawn from nature and on stone by W. Spreat, 1842.)

20. William Makepeace Thackeray (1811-63). (Photograph by E. Edwards, *c.*1863.)

1. A Consecration Cross in Ottery Church. It was restored y William Butterfield (1814-1900) in 1850.

22. Bernard, second Baron Coleridge (Mr. Justice Coleridge) by 'Spy'.

23. The King's School in The College. (Demolished in 1884.)

24. (*top*) Cadhay from the north-east. A courtyard manor-house of mixed Tudor and Georgian architecture.

25. (*centre*) Silver Street, Ottery St Mary, about 1903.

26. (*bottom*) Church Hill, Ottery St Mary, about 1912.

27. (*opposite above*) Church Hill (now called Silver Street) in the 1970s.

28. (*opposite below*) View of Ottery St Mary looking south-east towards East Hill.

29. The Church of St Mary by flood-light.

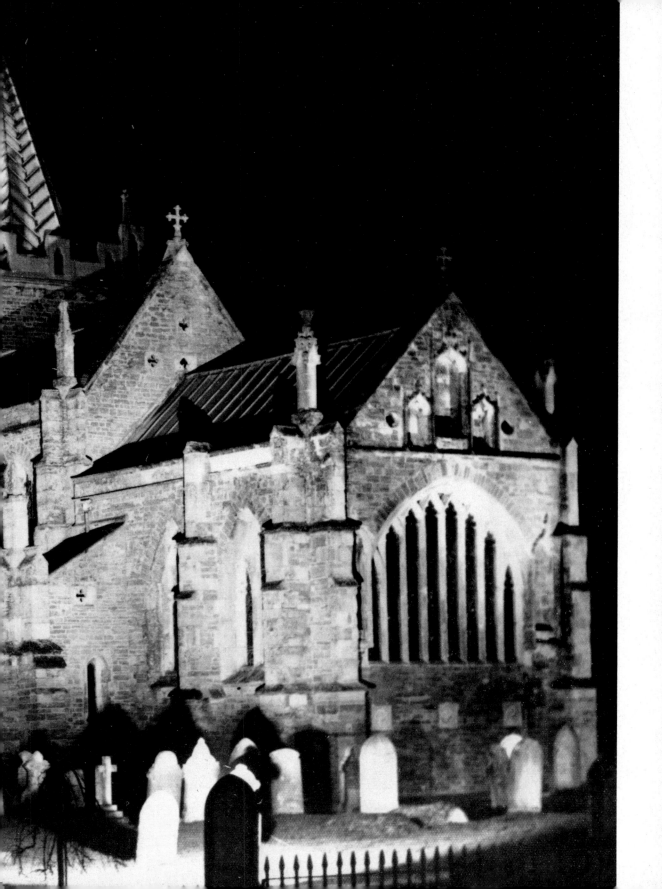

30.   Ottery St Mary Carnival: a flaming tar-barrel is hoisted shoulder-high (1983).

Apart from its great age of well over 600 years, this lectern has the distinction of being one of the few remaining wooden eagle lecterns in England. According to the late Sir Nikolaus Pevsner, 21 medieval wooden lecterns remain, but most of these are of the simple desk form.

Medieval paintings

The portrayal of religious subjects by wall paintings in an endeavour to teach in an age when books were rare and congregations often illiterate, was inspired work. It was during the 14th century that medieval painting reached its greatest glory. Professionalism in art had not yet been attained at the expense of inspiration. Medieval painted decoration was strictly conventional, yet bold in outline and somewhat primitive in colour, for 'at that date our own Countrymen had very little Idea of Art'.

The 20 panels which form the upper two tiers of Decorated arcading on the back, or eastern side, of the altar screen appear to have contained paintings depicting the Blessed Virgin Mary and Child, surrounded by the prophets. Each figure had a scroll bearing a name or some other inscription. A water-colour drawing by V. Bonner in 1792 shows that these paintings were executed with great delicacy in three colours—black, red and yellow. In an inscription attached to the interesting drawing, the artist explained that he could not pass by 'this compact and elegant specimen of the architect of its time' without drawing it for himself. He took special care in copying the delicate touches of the original paintings on the screen, which, in his words, ornamented this part of the church 'with a refined display of good Taste'. (*See* Plate 7.)

When the reredos of Exeter Cathedral was being erected in 1316–17, the records show that Nicholas, the painter and figure sculptor, was paid 2s. (10p) a week. Lesser painters received no more than 1s. 6d. (7½p), whilst Richard, who ground the colours to powder on a marble stone, was paid 1s. 0d. (5p) for a week's work.

It is possible that the panels between the four niches on the front of the minstrels' gallery were originally filled with paintings to present an impressive approach to the lady chapel, which was a natural addition to a collegiate church. On either side of the gallery are small chapels at the east end of the choir aisles, following the similar arrangement in Exeter Cathedral. These are known as the Martyrs' Chapels, being dedicated to St Lawrence and St Stephen respectively, although they may originally have been dedicated to other saints.[6]

Roof bosses

A few words must be added about the richly-coloured roof bosses. These have been described as 'the keystones of vaulting' and serve to conceal the intersection of the ribs.[7]

Midway between the high altar and the west door is the founder's boss, showing Bishop Grandisson in full pontifical vestments with his right hand raised in benediction. It is at the centre of a cross formed by the vaulting ribs of the crossing and at the four points of this cross are smaller bosses. These bear the arms of Bishop Grandisson; his uncle, Sir Otho de Grandisson (to be distinguished from his younger brother); Katharine de Montacute, Countess of Salisbury (the bishop's sister) and Hugh Courtenay, Earl of Devon (the bishop's 'Cousin Courtenay').

Along the centre of the vaulting of the chancel are five bosses, which, viewed from west to east, represent: (a) St John the Baptist; (b) the Presentation of the Virgin Mary by St Anne, her Mother; (c) the Annunciation: St Gabriel and the Virgin Mary; (d) the Blessed Virgin and Child; and (e) the Coronation of the Virgin Mary by Our Lord. The two bosses in the vaulting of the lady chapel represent the Blessed Virgin and Child, and Our Lord enthroned in glory.

Sir Otho de Grandisson and Lady Beatrix

On either side of the nave are the effigies of Sir Otho de Grandisson and his wife, Lady Beatrix, which rest beneath fine ogee-headed canopies, each containing 50 shields for arms, with cusping and richly-carved foliage. The recumbent figure of Sir Otho, a younger brother of the bishop, is on the north side, and displays workmanship of a high standard. He is represented in full armour with his head resting upon his helm. At his feet is a lion, the symbol of strength and vigilance.

Lady Beatrix, who survived her husband, was a daughter of Nicholas de Malmaynes. She had a son, Sir Thomas de Grandisson, who died in 1375, and a daughter, Elizabeth. Her effigy, which is on the south side of the nave, shows her in a plain full dress of the period, her hands resting on her breast, and her hair braided with a heavy roll on either side of her face. Her head is supported by the outspread wings of two angels, whilst at her feet are two dogs, the emblems of fidelity.

Sir Otho de Grandisson died on 23 May 1359 within two months of having made his will, by which he bequeathed his body to be buried in the collegiate church of 'St Mary de Otery in the diocese of Exeter, in case his death should occur there . . . desiring his friends and executors not to permit any armed men or horse to proceed before his corpse to his funeral, nor any cover over it of cloth of gold or flourisht work, or his Arms thereupon but only a white cloth with a red Cross'.

He expressed the wish that if his death should happen at Chelsfield in Kent, where his elder brother, Thomas de Grandisson (1293–1317), had been rector, then he should be buried in the Chapel of St John there. However, there is no record of Sir Otho, or his wife, having been buried at Chelsfield or, in fact, elsewhere in Kent, and in view of their resplendent memorials in Ottery church, there would appear to be ample reason to believe that they were buried here.

The collegiate buildings

Bishop Grandisson's Foundation included extensive buildings, which were grouped on three sides of the church. The octagonal chapter house stood close to the south transept (as is the case at Exeter Cathedral) and cloisters led from

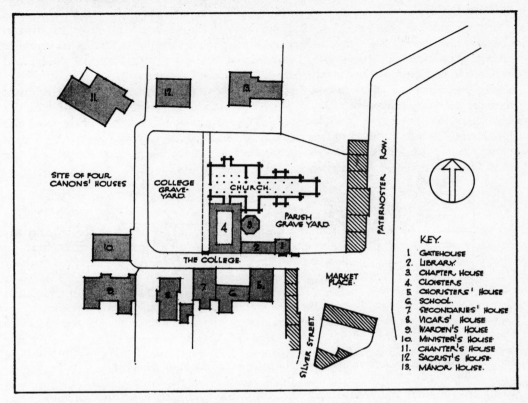

Fig. 4. Plan of the Collegiate Foundation (1337-1545).

the Vicars' House to where the south porch of the church now stands. The chapter house opened into these cloisters, which were described in an inventory of 1545 as being 54ft. long and 18ft. wide. (Fig. 4.)

College gate (or 'Mornt House' as it was later to be known) stood slightly to the west of the present main entrance to the churchyard at the top of Church Hill (now called Silver Street). The parishioners passed through the right-hand arch of the gateway into their part of the churchyard, whilst the clergy entered by another archway into the college close on the west side. The morn-priest, who kept the keys of the gate, resided in rooms above, and each night at curfew he closed the large oak gates.

At a later date a lychgate was added on the east side of the gatehouse. The Anglo-Saxon word *lych* meant 'a corpse', and it was at funerals that the coffin was rested on a wooden or stone table under this roofed gateway to await the clergy, and the lychgate also served to shelter the bearers and mourners during the first part of the burial service, which took place there.

College gate was considerably restored in Tudor times, and the arms of the see of Exeter, which had been displayed above the archways, were altered by Bishop Hugh Oldham of Exeter (1504-19).

Fig. 5.   The gatehouse (known as 'Mornt House'), where the morn priest of
               the college resided.

Both the ancient gatehouse and the adjoining lychgate were in existence until early in the last century.

On the west side of the gate was the college library, a considerable building, which was entered from the west end, and was about 50ft. in length, with six small windows facing south. On 28 July 1445, Canon John of Exeter bequeathed to the college some 136 books for this library. These would have been chained to the shelves in a similar manner to the books still to be seen in the library of Hereford Cathedral, and also at Wimborne Minster, as they were rare and of great value in those times.

The clergy-houses stood in orderly array within the precincts of the collegiate church. On the south side of the road now known as 'The College' was the choristers' hospice, and adjoining this was the school for the choirboys (which in 1545 became the King's New Grammar School). Beyond, was the Secondaries' House, where the eight clerks resided, then came the Vicars' House, and it was here that the eight vicars choral lived. Today, it continues to be known as The Vicars' House, with the apostrophe shown after the 's', although only one vicar now lives there.

Near the south-west corner of the churchyard was the Warden's House, where the senior canon resided. This house still exists, although much altered.

Along the west side, beyond the churchyard were, first, the Minister's House (he being one of the four senior canons) and then came four detached houses for each of the minor canons. These houses have long since disappeared, and their sites now form part of the grounds of the Chanter's House, which stands at the north-west corner of the churchyard (*see* Chapter Eleven). Next was the Sacrist's House, and he was entrusted with the care of the sacred vessels of the church, and also with looking after the books and vestments. Finally came the Manor Hall, where the manorial courts were held and the secular business of the parish was conducted (*see* Chapters Eight and Eleven).

The Black Death, 1348–50

By this time much of the Otter valley had been drained, and the land cleared of forest and scrub, and put under cultivation. Ottery St Mary was the centre of a farming community, although the tenants held their land under what was still essentially a feudal system.

In August 1348 the bubonic plague, which had swept Europe, reached the Dorset coast.[8] This pestilence was borne by fleas carried on black rats brought to this country by merchant ships, and, being of a highly contagious nature, it soon reached Devon and most other parts of England. Rich and poor alike were struck down, and died within a few days. Nearly half the population became victims of the dread disease. Farms were left abandoned and soon became derelict and overgrown for need of tenants. Entire families were wiped out by what became known as 'the Black Death'. This virulent plague remained as a constant threat, which most villages and small towns had to face for the next 300 years, for it was to recur from time to time.

Early chapelries

In the Middle Ages there were few bridges, for the building of these was a costly and difficult undertaking. Rivers and streams had to be crossed at places where they could be forded, or a ferry was available. Many of our place-names adopt the suffix -bridge or -ford, which has retained its original meaning of 'a crossing-place'. These elements are usually coupled with some distinctive topographical or other characteristic. Hence, we have Fenny Bridge, or 'the bridge over the marshy land'. Such names as Taleford, meaning 'the ford across the River Tale' and Gosford, meaning 'the goose ford' are examples to be found near Ottery St Mary.

But the crossing of rivers presented serious difficulties until the Church, which looked after the welfare of travellers, recognised that the building and maintenance of bridges was essential work, worthy of the support of pious donors. In course of time, it became the practice to grant special religious indulgences and absolutions to those persons who, either by their manual efforts or by gifts of money, contributed towards the building or repair of bridges and roads. Bequests of money were sometimes made by will for this purpose.

A small chapel might be built near the river-crossing or incorporated in the actual structure of the bridge itself, so that masses could be said for the repose of the donor's soul. The provision of such chapels along his route met the needs of the wayfarer, for here he could rest and offer prayers for his safety.

An entry dated 1 June 1355 in the Register of Bishop John de Grandisson (vol. I, p. 185) records that he had built a chapel 'on the Bridge of Ottery', which was dedicated to Our Saviour. On 8 September 1438 Bishop Edmund Lacy (1420–55) granted an indulgence of 40 days for the repair of this chapel and the bridge.

Priests or lay-hermits were often entrusted with the charge of bridges and ferries, and there is an entry dated 9 November 1531 in Bishop John Veysey's Register (1519–51) in which it is stated that he had permitted John Selman to become a lay-hermit at Our Saviour's Chapel at Ottery. Among the duties of the lay-hermit, or recluse, would be the collection of tolls for the maintenance of the bridge from those wayfarers who used it.

There was a chapel of St Budeaux on the east side of the town in Yonder Street, but the date of this is not known. Although these chapels have long since disappeared, the names 'St Saviour's', and 'St Budeaux' still survive for their particular localities. It would seem that at some period of its history the town was divided into three districts: Ottery St Mary's, Ottery St Budeaux, and Ottery St Saviour's.

At the ancient mansions of Holcombe and Knightstone there were also small private chapels, of which some remains may still be seen (*see* Chapter Eleven).

Grandisson prohibits Christmas plays in churches

Religious plays were originally performed in the Church by the lower orders of the clergy, who were assisted by choir-boys chanting in Latin. These plays were a way of portraying biblical stories, for very few people were able to read. In the Middle Ages, mystery and miracle plays were increasing in popularity, but they were also tending to attract an undesirable element within the precincts of the Church. The religious aspect was becoming subsidiary, and, as Sir Ifor Evans has aptly expressed the position, 'the element of devotion decreased as the element of dramatic presentation increased'.[9] When the main object of the play became to amuse, this was soon to lead to profanity.

Early in December 1360, Bishop Grandisson issued a prohibition to the warden and canons at Ottery St Mary against the performance of plays in the church at Christmas. The clergy agreed to read the bishop's mandate at all services and to stop such performances. And so these liturgical plays were moved from the precincts of the church to the market-place, to fairs or inn-yards, where they were performed on open wooden platforms erected for the purpose. In course of time, the subject-matter widened as the plays became more secular, and led to the beginning of English drama.

Death of John de Grandisson

John de Grandisson died on 15 July 1369 in his 77th year, after an episcopate of 42 years. His great work of beautifying his beloved cathedral at Exeter was completed, and he had achieved his ambition by founding his college of canons at Ottery St Mary.

He was buried in the mortuary chapel of St Radegundes within the image-wall, which forms a screen masking the buttresses of the west front of the cathedral.

On the ceiling of this small chapel was sculptured Christ in Glory, so positioned that, in accordance with medieval tradition, it would meet the bishop's gaze on the Day of Resurrection.

It is sad to relate that in the reign of Elizabeth I, some 200 years later, Bishop Grandisson's tomb was desecrated, and his 'ashes scattered abroad and the bones bestowed no man knoweth where'.[10]

Games in churchyards

In the Middle Ages sports were played with vigorous abandon, as they were not controlled by any written rules and there was seldom any organisation. The result was that games frequently deteriorated into rowdyism, and even brawling.

There is evidence of tennis being played early in this period, and balls banged against the church walls to the distraction of the clergy and their congregations, and occasionally windows were broken. Yet many of the clergy themselves took an active part in these games, although secretly!

It is recorded that in August 1451, the canons and their lay friends of Ottery St Mary played tennis within the precincts of the collegiate church, when it had been forbidden by the bishop.

A letter of prohibition contained in the Register of Edmund Lacy, Bishop of Exeter, stated:[11]

> By vain, foul and prophane words, by senseless and swelling oaths, by torrents of unlawful perjuries, they shamelessly occasioned such brawling, contention and yelling in the sacred churchyard that the devotions of Christian people coming there to pray for souls departed were vilely and damnably disturbed.

The Dean and Chapter of Exeter complained to the mayor, who, unable to prevent the playing of games in the Cathedral Close, appealed to the king. He took the view that as tennis was interfering with archery, it must be prohibited. Edward IV (1461-83) banned the game, and this prohibition was to be repeated by both Henry VII and Henry VIII.

Bishop Edmund Lacy had paid a visit to the college at Ottery St Mary on 8 September 1437 and been entertained by the warden and canons. He stayed the night there, and the cost of entertaining him amounted to 13s. 10½d. (69p), which was quite a large sum in those days.

In July 1451, the college was visited by Henry VI, who was received with great solemnity by the warden, John Hancock, and the other canons. The king spent two nights as their guest.

The Bonvilles of Shute

The de Bonvilles came from Normandy during the 12th century and settled in south-east Devon. The family bought Wiscombe in the next century and made a deer park there, but it was not until about 1380 that they built the splendid medieval manor-house of Shute, which they made their principal residence.

Sir William de Bonville (or Boneville) became Sheriff of Dorset and Somerset in 1381 and 1382, and was made Sheriff of Devon in 1390. He endowed a hospital for 12 poor men and women in Exeter, and this benefaction is still recalled by a plaque, which may be seen in the Lunt Homes there. The de Bonvilles became powerful landowners and were formidable rivals of the Courtenays, who resided at Colcombe Castle, Colyton.

As Sir William's eldest son, John, had predeceased him in 1396, the Bonville estates passed to his grandson, William, who was born at Shute on 31 August 1392. He became Sheriff of Devon in 1422, and, being created Lord Bonville and Chewton, was summoned to parliament from 1449 until 1460. By his first wife, Margaret, he had a son, William, who married the daughter and sole heiress of William, Lord Harington, K.G., and by right of his wife he took the title of 6th Lord Harington. His son married Catherine, daughter of Richard Neville, Earl of Salisbury, and by her he had a daughter, Cicely, born in 1460. Through her mother she was a direct descendant of Katharine, Countess of Salisbury, the sister of Bishop Grandisson, and could also trace her descent back to John of Gaunt, the third son of Edward III.

It was Lady Cicely's misfortune to be born at a time when a bitter struggle was being waged between the powerful landed families with the Crown of England as the main objective. The series of battles, which were to be known as the Wars of the Roses, were of increasing ferocity; Lady Cicely was only a few months old when both her father, himself still under age, and her grandfather, William Bonville, 6th Lord Harington, were killed at the Battle of Wakefield (31 December 1460).

Less than two months later, her great-grandfather, William, Lord Bonville and Chewton, was betrayed after the second Battle of St Albans, and beheaded. Upon the violent extinction of the male line of the Bonvilles their estates and possessions in the West Country passed to the infant Lady Cicely as sole heiress. She took the title of Baroness Harington, Bonville and Chewton.

In 1476 at the age of 16 she married Thomas Grey, 1st Marquess of Dorset, who was the elder son of the queen, Elizabeth Woodville, by her first marriage. The early years of Lady Cicely's married life were fraught with difficulties because her husband, as a member of the unpopular Woodville family, was deeply involved in the bitter feuds.

The medieval manor house of Knightstone (*Knyghtestone*) to the south of Ottery St Mary passed to her in 1494 on the death of Richard Bittlesgate without issue, and her husband held the property in her right and did homage for it to the manor of Ottery. Knightstone was ultimately to merge in the estates of the marquesses of Dorset, where it continued until 1553 (*see* Chapter Eleven).

Perkin Warbeck: Exeter under siege

Early in September 1497 insurrection was astir in the South-West. Perkin Warbeck, who claimed he was Prince Richard, Duke of York, the younger of the two princes reputed to have been murdered in the Tower, crossed over from Ireland and landed on the Cornish coast near Penzance. After taking St Michael's

Mount, he proclaimed himself 'King Richard IV' at Bodmin and, encouraged by his success, he decided to march against Exeter. On reaching the walls of the city, he had gathered a rebel army of about 6,000 men. Believing the west gate, which was the main entrance, to be impregnable, he decided to attack the north gate, but, after setting this on fire, his army was repulsed.

A heavier attack was then launched against the east gate, which was smashed down, and Warbeck fought his way into the city, but was soon driven out again after some bitter hand-to-hand fighting. Although the attack was renewed the next morning, Warbeck realised that he could not take Exeter, and so decided to withdraw on the best terms he could get. He attempted to flee the country, but soon found that all means of escape were closed to him.

Meanwhile, Henry VII had arrived at Taunton, and it was here that Perkin Warbeck was compelled to seek the king's mercy and make a public confession of his imposture.

The king came on to Exeter where he stayed at the house of the cathedral treasurer, which then adjoined the north tower. From an upper window he graciously pardoned the rebel prisoners, who were assembled before him in the Cathedral Yard, bare-headed, dressed merely in their shirts, and with halters round their necks, expecting to be hanged. In thanking the citizens of Exeter for their faithful and valiant service, the king presented to the mayor, John Atwill, a Sword of State, together with a Cap of Maintenance of black beaver in recognition of the city's loyalty. These are still carried before the mayor on all ceremonial occasions.

The rebellion having been successfully subdued, Henry VII decided to visit his brother-in-law, Thomas Grey, at Shute, where he stayed for a week. Whilst there, he went to the lovely Cistercian abbey of Newenham, set in pastoral surroundings on the banks of the river Axe, south-west of Axminster. On his way to Shute, the king came to Ottery St Mary on 3 November 1497, and was entertained by the warden and canons of the college. He spent the night there as their royal guest.

The 'Dorset' aisle

During her 19 years as the wife of Thomas Grey, Marquess of Dorset, who died in 1501, Lady Cicely bore him seven sons and eight daughters. She remarried in 1503, her second husband being Henry, Lord Stafford, Earl of Wiltshire, who was a younger son of Henry, Duke of Buckingham. On his death in 1523 without issue, his title became extinct.

It was due to the munificence of Lady Cicely that there was built the beautiful fan-vaulted 'Dorset' aisle, which she added to the collegiate church in 1519–20. Her descent from the Grandisson family was possibly an inducement to enlarge and beautify this church. The fan-vault was a distinctive feature of the Perpendicular Gothic style of English architecture, which had a brief late revival in the South-West.

The original north wall of the nave was removed, and an arcade of five arches erected, carried by clustered piers. The rich beauty of the fan-vaults is an outstanding feature of the church, and from the centre of the vaulting five large pendant bosses of open tracery terminate in Tudor roses.

The decoration of the pier-capitals consists of foliage, and ribbon-work, and among the latter is an exquisitely carved elephant's head (Plate 10). Another noticeable feature of the Dorset aisle, so-named after Lady Cicely's title as Marchioness of Dorset, is the heraldic decoration, both inside and on the external walls. Stafford knots, frets, and mullets, representative of her family, appear in the mouldings.

At the western end of the arcade are two owls, which form pier-cap decoration, the emblems of Hugh Oldham, Bishop of Exeter (1504–19), whilst in the south-east corner a demi-angel holds an heraldic shield displaying the arms of his successor, Bishop John Veysey (1519–51), significantly placing the date when this aisle was added. On a summer evening, with the sun behind the large west window, the fan tracery assumes a mellow beauty in which shades of Tudor England seem to linger.

Lady Cicely was also responsible for additions to other churches of parishes in which she owned property, such as Axminster and Seaton.

By her will, dated 6 May 1527, she expressed the wish to be buried with her first husband at 'the new Chapel of Our Lady in the College of Astley'.[12] She is described as 'Cicile, Marquess Dorset, Lady Harington and Bonville, later wife of the Marquis Dorset'.

Alexander Barclay (1475?–1552)

Most people are familiar with such sayings as 'robbing Peter to pay Paul', 'of two evils choose the least', or 'out of sight, out of mind', but they seldom know where or when these sayings originated. Other expressions such as 'skin deep', 'from pillar to post', or 'making the mouth water' are in daily use, yet they find their origin in the works of Alexander Barclay, a scholar and poet, writing in the early 16th century.

After being educated at Oxford, he was appointed chaplain to the collegiate church at Ottery St Mary by his friend, Thomas Cornyssh, who was warden there from 1490 until 1511. Alexander Barclay was responsible for introducing the pastoral into English poetry in his short dialogue poems, but he is chiefly remembered for the *Ship of Fools* (1509), which was a free translation into English verse of Sebastian Brandt's *Narrenschiff*, which had been written in the Swabian dialect some 15 years earlier. This work had won fame in Europe, and Alexander Barclay's skilful adaptation gives a

Fig. 6. A 16th-century agricultural labourer. (A woodcut from Alexander Barclay's *Fifte Eglog*.)

satirical picture of contemporary life in England. The *Ship of Fools* exposes the follies and vices of man, and all fools are shipped off to the Land of Fools, where they more properly belong. By producing one of the great books in the English language, into which he added much original work and literary skill, Alexander Barclay helped to fill the gap in our literature of that period.

After his time as a priest and scholar at Ottery St Mary he became a monk at Ely, and died at Croydon in 1552.

The 'bare ruined choirs'

The Reformation cast an ominous shadow over the monastic system in England. For a long time the number of monks and friars had been declining as enthusiasm for monasticism waned and a secular way of life took over.

On 3 July 1534, Oliver Smyth, the warden of the college of St Mary of Ottery, supported by Roger Bramston, the minister, Roger Stokeman, the sacristan, and William Dyeher, one of the canons, took the oath subscribing to the king's supremacy by upholding the validity of his marriage to Anne Boleyn and rejecting the authority of the Pope.

Many monasteries had already surrendered when the Suppression of the Lesser Monasteries Act of 1536 brought about the dissolution of nearly 400 of the smaller religious houses whose incomes were less than £200. Although it was conceded that in the greater houses 'religion is right well kept and observed', the clouds were rapidly gathering. In spite of its pretext to be a measure of reform, it was soon clear that the Act was designed to fill the coffers of the Crown, although much of the monastic land was shortly to be transferred into other hands.

Altar plate, jewellery, magnificently embroidered vestments and other treasures of the religious houses were carried off by the Commissioners 'for the King's use', and lead was stripped from the roofs to be sold or melted down.

The time may have come for monasticism to go, and the monks and friars, living in easy comfort and worldliness upon the accumulated endowments of a past age, may have outlived their noble heritage. But this could not excuse the tyrannical and avaricious plundering of the monasteries, and after them the chantries, that went on throughout the country.

As certain insurrections failed, notably the Pilgrimage of Grace during the closing months of 1536, pressure was brought to induce 'voluntary' surrenders of the greater religious houses, which increased apace. With only three such surrenders in 1537, there were no less than 174 in 1539. An Act of Parliament was passed in that latter year confirming the surrenders to that time, and it was extended to all remaining religious houses. For Bishop Grandisson's splendid college the days were numbered. The last warden, John Ffysher, prepared to surrender after holding office for barely six months.

Chapter Five

DISSOLUTION OF THE COLLEGE

THE WARDEN and canons of the college at Ottery St Mary surrendered on 28 May 1545. Two days later, the king's commissioners made an inventory of 'all the plate jewells, ornaments, goods and cattalles apperteiginge to the late surrendered College of Our blessed Lady of Ottery in the County of Devon'.

In his *History of England,* the late Professor G. M. Trevelyan expressed the view that 'The wealth of the monasteries and after them of the chantries, should have gone to multiply and enlarge the schools formerly attached to a few of the monasteries and many of the chantries'. Instead, the inventory relating to the college stated: 'according to the King's Majesty's Commission, all plate, ornaments, goods, cattalls, bells, glass, yeron [iron] and lead was delivered to the custodie of Mathew Colhurste, and Humfrey Coles, Esquires, to be reserved to the King's Majesties' use unto suche tyme as his Grace's pleaser be furder knowen therein'. Furthermore, as the result of the dissolution of the greater religious houses up and down the country, priceless treasures of learning and art of several centuries were being wantonly destroyed or dispersed.

On 7 October 1547, in accordance with the directions of his father's will, Edward VI granted the endowments[1] of the collegiate foundation and the great tithes of the parish to the dean and canons of St George's Chapel, Windsor. The annual revenue then amounted to £338 2s. 9d. (£338.14), which was a considerable sum in those days.

By Letters Patent under the Great Seal of England dated 24 December 1545, Henry VIII 'for the universal good and common advantage of all and every the inhabitants of the parish of St Mary of Ottery' decreed that four of such inhabitants for the time being should be incorporated by the name of 'The Four Governors of the Hereditaments and Goods of the Church of St Mary, Ottery in the County of Devon', and that they should have succession for ever. The first governors were John Haydon of Cadhay, William Sherman of Knightstone, Hugh More, and William Trent.[2] The king vested in these four governors the church, the churchyard with the belfry, and the chapel named Our Lady's Chapel, the vestries, the cloisters, and the chapter house, with their appurtenances, lately belonging to the college. Likewise, there were vested in the governors the various clergy houses, known as the Vicars' House, the Secondaries' House, the Choristers' House and the Schoolhouse.[3] In addition, the governors were to have the small tithes of the parish. The property, and these tithes, were of a clear annual value of £45 19s. 2d. (£45.96). On the dissolution, the great collegiate church became a parish church. (The total number of religious foundations which suffered spoliation during the last years of Henry VIII and the first of his son, Edward VI, was estimated at upwards of three thousand.) The vicar of Ottery St Mary was to be nominated by the Crown, and paid £20 a year by the governors at Lady Day and Michaelmas in equal portions. Henry VIII founded a free grammar school to endure for ever, and to be known as the King's School (*see* Chapter Six). There were to be two chaplain priests, but it was later (1598) agreed that it would be in order should the governors think one to be sufficient.

Assistant governors (1552)

But all did not go well for the governors. The parishioners were soon to find cause for complaint, and in 1552 they commenced a suit in the Court of Augmentations.[4] A settlement was reached with the approval of the court whereby, under articles dated 20 October 1552, Edward VI required the governors, on the advice of the parishioners, with convenient speed to 'elect, nominate and appoint eight others of the most honest, best, discreetest and quietest of the parishioners' to assist them in doing all such things 'as should seem best to their wisdom and discretion for the wealth, profit and behoof of the whole parishioners'.

These eight assistants were to aid the governors in dealing with financial matters, and 'for the better maintenance of the Divine Service of God and doing of deeds of charity for the Relief of the Poor within the said Parish as occasion from time to time should serve . . .'.

Destruction of the chapter house and the cloister

It was not long after the dissolution of the college that the chapter house, which adjoined the south transept, and the cloister leading from the Vicars' House, were pulled down, and the building-stone and other materials exposed for pillage. Some of the stone was most likely taken and used by John Haydon, who at that time was engaged in building at Cadhay 'a fair new house'.[5] (*See* Chapter Eleven.)

The cloister had led into the church on the south side of the nave, but now a porch was added to which John Haydon carried out some later work. His arms are displayed over the entrance, and his initials 'J.H. 1571' may be discerned on the plate of the iron ring on the south door. In ancient characters above the door may be deciphered the words:

> He that no Il will do
> Do nothyng yt lang yto.
> Anno Domino 1571.

(He that does no ill, does nothing that belongs thereto.)

Battle of Fenny Bridges: 27 July 1549

The country was in a state of religious turmoil, and in much of Devon and Cornwall the peasantry, resentful of change, clung loyally to the old faith. They were incensed when the first Act of Uniformity was passed on 1 January 1549 abolishing the use of the old Latin mass, and directing that the new English prayer book be introduced on the following Whit Sunday. They regarded this as an encroachment into their traditional way of life, and were soon to rise in open rebellion.

The trouble started at Sampford Courtenay, an attractive Devon village on the northern fringe of Dartmoor, where the parishioners refused to accept the revised form of prayer book, and compelled their priest to don his vestments and celebrate mass in the old form. Tactless handling of this inflammatory situation by the local magistrates turned intense anger into violence, and fanned the sparks of rebellion into flame.

Many Cornishmen who were also provoked at having the unwanted prayer book forced upon them, joined the cause, and before long there were 10,000 men in arms. Lord Protector Somerset sent Sir Peter Carew and his brother, Sir Gawen Carew of Mohuns Ottery, near Luppitt, to meet the catholic rebels, who had by then reached Crediton, and attempt to reason with them and hear their grievances. But the Carews were intolerant, and instead of negotiating with the rebels, they inflamed matters still further.

By 2 July Exeter was under siege, and the gates of the city were closed against the rebels. Although many of the leading citizens were ardent catholics, including the mayor, they had no wish to become involved in this insurrection, and refused to yield. Instead of pressing on with their eastward march and possibly gathering further support, the insurgents lost valuable time attempting to capture the city. This delay enabled Lord Russell, who had been appointed to suppress the insurrection, to reach Honiton with an army consisting mainly of Italian and German mercenaries.

When an advance party of the rebels eventually reached Fenny Bridge, which spanned the river Otter some four miles west of Honiton, Lord Russell was awaiting the arrival of Lord Grey de Wilton with mercenary reinforcements from Oxfordshire. However, the presence of the rebels at Fenny Meadow posed a direct threat to Honiton. They were encamped to the north of the road and had the protection of rising ground behind them, whilst before them was the river Otter.

The impulsive Sir Peter Carew advised an immediate attack without waiting further for Lord Grey and his army, and to this proposal Lord Russell readily agreed. And so, after Sir Peter and his brother had cleared the way, but not without some fierce resistance during which Sir Gawen was shot through the arm, Lord Russell brought up his army from Honiton, and on 27 July 1549 the ferocious battle of Fenny Bridge took place. It started with a bitter skirmish, the rebels being forced to give way. Russell's foreign mercenaries, thinking that victory was theirs, became undisciplined, and searched for plunder and spoil.

But the catholic rebels, who had numbered several hundred, had been awaiting a Cornish force to join them. At this point in the battle they arrived, and Lord Russell's pillaging mercenaries were taken by surprise. A fierce struggle ensued and the foreign mercenaries suffered severely, many being cut to pieces. John Hooker, an Exeter contemporary historian wrote: 'The fight for the time was very sharp and cruel, for the Cornishmen were very lusty and fresh, and fully bent to fight out the matter'. In the end, the more experienced fighters won through, and Lord Russell's soldiers managed to extricate themselves. They rallied and drove the rebels from the field, leaving 300 dead, but it is likely that their own losses in men had been as great as that of the rebels.

Cautiously, Lord Russell returned to Honiton to reorganise his battered forces, and it was not until a week later (Saturday, 3 August) that he set off over the high ground towards Woodbury Common. Wherever possible he kept away from roads as he was anxious to avoid any clashes on ground not of his own choosing.

Although the tragic closing stages of the Western Rebellion may not strictly form part of Ottery's story, some brief mention of them should be made to conclude this account. Lord Russell's army camped for the night on Woodbury Common near a windmill, the mound of which may still be seen beside the road. Whilst there, a small rebel force came up from Clyst St Mary, and there was another fierce skirmish with heavy loss of life.

The next day Lord Russell and his royalist army moved towards the hard-pressed city of Exeter, and a bitter and furious battle took place on Clyst Heath above Clyst St Mary, which commanded a wide view of the surrounding country. Once more the catholic rebels fought with outstanding bravery, but this was to prove the turning point of the 'Prayer Book' rebellion, for about 4,000 men were killed: '. . . great was the slaughter and cruel was the fight'.

The royalist army had achieved a decisive victory, and after a siege which had lasted for over five weeks and food supplies had become low causing the citizens to suffer considerable hardship, Exeter was relieved on 6 August. A brutal retribution followed, and the disorganised remnants of the rebel army returned to Sampford Courtenay. Even at this late stage the rebels put up a last desperate fight in the narrow village streets, but were soon overpowered by superior forces.

The Cornish ring-leaders were 'hanged, drawn and quartered' at Tyburn, and gallows were erected in Devon and Cornwall for other rebels to meet a similar fate. These catholic peasants were prepared to die for a cause they held just, but their rebellion had been destined to failure from the start; they had fought bravely against insuperable odds.

'One greate bell'

There had been a peal of eight bells in the collegiate church, four in the north or parish tower, and a like number in the south or college tower, for the tolling of which Bishop Grandisson had prescribed in his Statutes careful instructions. But as a result of the Western Rebellion, the church bells in Devonshire were melted down, saving only 'the least of the ring'.[6]

An inventory made in 1553 mentioned that there was 'one greate bell' remaining in the church at Ottery St Mary. Today there is a ring of eight bells again, but all of these hang in the south tower. The oldest is dated 1652.

Queen Elizabeth I's visitors

In 1559, Queen Elizabeth I's commissioners carried out further desecration. The empty niches throughout the church tell their own sad story. The beautiful altar screen was defaced by their order, and the original niches and canopies were 'hewen down and afterwards made a playne walle with morter and plaster'. By chopping off all the projecting work on the altar screen, and filling the many niches with mortar, the whole was made to present 'a tolerably smooth surface for the plasterer'.

We have some indication of the ruthless behaviour of the queen's visitors at Exeter, where it was recorded 'they defaced and pulled down and burnt in the Cathedral Yard all the images and monuments they could find, and among other things defaced the Altars'. In a letter of 1560, the queen instructed her visitors to determine some means of reformation, 'and among other things to order that the tables of the Commandments may be comlye set or hung up in the east end of the Chauncell'.

Immediately above the table (the altar having been removed in accordance with an Act of 1549) were placed the ten commandments in two compartments. With the exception of the fourth commandment, which was abbreviated, the other commandments were set out in full in ancient lettering of a reddish hue. Painted pilasters, of the same height as the screen, were added later on either side of the commandments, and above all were placed the royal arms.[7]

It was during these troublous years that Gervase Babington was born at Ottery St Mary, and rose to become Bishop of Exeter in 1595. Two years later he was translated to Worcester, and died in 1610.

Inspeximus

On 18 March 1574, the governors obtained an Inspeximus of the Letters Patent under which the church corporation had been founded by Henry VIII. This was an attested copy of the charter, the Latin word 'Inspeximus' meaning 'we have inspected or looked at'. It provided the governors with confirmation under the great seal, as the original Letters Patent appear to have been lost.

The Spanish Armada

In the third week of July 1588, the mighty Spanish Armada sailed up the English Channel, harassed and pursued by the small ships of Lord Howard of Effingham. On the southern extremity of Ottery's East Hill a beacon was lit to pass on the alarm by a chain of flares across the breadth of England. With the Spanish fleet off the coast of Devon, there would have been great excitement in Ottery St Mary, and by 22 July it sailed past Sidmouth on its way from The Lizard to Calais, and eventual destruction by storms and shipwreck, as every schoolboy knows.

Assistants v. Governors

The conduct of the governors gave cause for further complaint, for which the religious turmoil of the times was partly responsible. Furthermore, there seems to have been constant discord between them and the assistants.

Under the Letters Patent the governors were required to fill any vacancy in their number by electing one of the assistants within one month of such vacancy arising. It appears, however, that they were deliberately failing to do this, which meant that it was the duty of the vicar to appoint a new governor. Instead of electing one from the assistants, he had accepted a bribe and had been appointing other persons, whose names were put to him.

In 1598 an action was brought by two of the assistants against the governors and the vicar (the Rev. Nicholas Forward) in the Court of Exchequer, charging them with appointing one, Antony Saunders, as schoolmaster, when he was 'a known and noted Papist', granting him £10 a year, and 'with other malpractices to the great prejudice of the inhabitants of the parish'. A decree was made by the court expelling the four governors, and precluding them from re-election!

Galleries

In concluding this chapter, mention must be made of the damage to the church when the nave was disfigured by ugly galleries early in the 17th century. A part of the beautiful canopy over the recumbent effigy of Lady Beatrix de Grandisson was cut off to enable a gallery to be built above the south aisle. The desire for galleries at this period led to three more being erected in the transepts.

Chapter Six

'THE KYNGE'S NEW GRAMMER SCOLE'

ON THE DISSOLUTION of the college, Henry VIII founded a free grammar school 'to endure always for all time to come', and ordained that it should be called 'the Kynge's Newe Grammer Scole of Seynt Marie Oterey'. It was, in fact, a continuation of the former choir school, which had been part of the collegiate foundation. But it was characteristic of Henry VIII that he should claim credit for that which he liked to consider his own foundation, irrespective of whether it was little more than a variation or extension of an existing endowment.

He wished it to be known that he had founded this grammar school out of 'the particular love and affection with which we greatly favour the young subjects of our Kingdom within our said County of Devon', and added that it was for their instruction 'in more polite learning than before our time they were accustomed'.

A master was to be appointed from time to time by the four church governors and the vicar, and be paid an annual salary of £10 'to instruct the youth of the parish'. If he should be absent from the school for the space of one month, he could be removed, and another schoolmaster appointed in his place. The governors were required to provide both the vicar and schoolmaster with 'a convenient habitation', and were to be responsible for the repair and maintenance of such houses for ever. The vicar resided in the Vicars' House of the former college, and what had been the Secondaries' House, which adjoined on the east side, now became the School House.

In June 1587, the school and 13 houses 'in the uppermost part of the towne' were seriously damaged by fire. John Haydon of Cadhay, as one of the church governors, was largely responsible for restoring the school and 'did forthwyth cause the same to be erected with as much speed convenyent as in such case might be required, disbursing and defraying the money thereof'. Unfortunately, he died in March the following year before the work had been completed, but the will of his widow, Joanna Haydon, tells us that he had spent 'above the sum of fortie pounds' on the rebuilding.

An early master, Antony Saunders, was expelled in 1598, for being 'a known and noted Papist', and was succeeded by Thomas Passemer, who continued until 1618. These are the first masters of whom there is any record.

Over the centuries the fortunes of the school have fluctuated, and at one low ebb when Richard Marker, B.A., was the master (1699-1730), he 'reduced this most flourishing school to be without one scholar', and was eventually compelled to resign. Among more successful masters was John Ball, M.A. (1636-51), who

36

was voted an additional £8 a year because he had 'beene a meanes to increase the number of schollers more than formerly had been, which is for the general good of the parish, and in regard he is at the charge of maintaining an usher'. An usher or assistant teacher became necessary when John Ball was also headmaster of the Free Grammar School at Exeter from 1642 until 1648.

On his death in 1651, he was succeeded by William Birstall, M.A., 'late Schoolmaster of Blandford in the County of Dorset'. Although he was appointed at a salary of £10 a year, the governors decided to pay him £13 6s. 8d. (£13.33), with '20s. [£1] more to his mayde', and a further £3 5s. 0d. (£3.25) for work done about the school. He resigned in 1655, but it was not until four years later that arrears of salary amounting to £2 were paid to him and, in addition, he was given a monetary award and a bond for £17 10s. 0d. (£17.50).

In 1662 Greaves Austin, M.A., became master, and held the appointment until his death nearly forty years later. He had been a student of Christ Church, Oxford, and under his headship the King's School flourished 'he having for many years together near 200 scholars under his care . . .'.

On 20 August 1760 the church governors, under the chairmanship of William Peere Williams of Cadhay, appointed the Rev. John Coleridge, B.A., master at a salary of £10 a year. He came to Ottery St Mary from South Molton in North Devon, where he had been master of Squire's Endowed Latin School. Whilst there he held a curacy at the small hamlet of Mariansleigh,[1] and was priested at Exeter Cathedral in December 1750. Four months after his appointment as master of the King's School, he became vicar of Ottery St Mary, and held both positions until his death in 1781.

John Coleridge has been described as 'an exceedingly studious man, pious, of primitive manners, and of the most simple habits; passing events were little heeded by him, and therefore he was usually characterized as "the absent man".'[2] During his short time at Cambridge he had taught himself Hebrew, and later he would frequently quote the scriptures in the original Hebrew, declaring to his incredulous parishioners that he would give them 'the immediate language of the Holy Ghost'.[3]

He was succeeded by two inefficient headmasters, so that when his son, the Rev. George Coleridge, B.A., was appointed in 1794 'for so long as he shall behave himself and faithfully discharge the said office', he found the school in a lamentable plight due to their neglect. He reported that 'the School of late years [1771–94] had only been formally kept up, there might be one or two scholars; . . . the premises were in a ruinous state, and the schoolroom was used for keeping rabbits and poultry'. During his 14 years as master he succeeded under his careful teaching and strict discipline in raising the standard of the school again, and increasing the number of scholars by 150 admissions.

His nephew, the Rev. Edward Coleridge (1800–83), had been sent to the school at an early age, and was later to say that his uncle had gained for the school 'the reputation of being the best in the West of England'. In an autobiography, Edward Coleridge told of the Spartan conditions at the school when he was a pupil in the early years of the 19th century.

The bell sounded at 5.30 a.m., and the pupils had to assemble in the school room, which was unheated, by 6.a.m. The master entered promptly and took prayers. During the winter months, tallow candles were placed on the desks by melting the ends. Under this personal discomfort, the pupils worked until 8 a.m. If they came ill-prepared and unable to answer questions correctly, this meant a caning on the hand, which the master grimly called 'Yellow Soap for Dirty Fingers'. After breakfast, there was usually time for a game 'at Prison Bars in the Long Walk of the Churchyard, where there were two rows of stately Elms'.

The pupils were back in the school again from 10 a.m. until 12 noon, and dinner was at 1 p.m. There were lessons in writing and arithmetic from 2 p.m. to 5 p.m., when old Simmonds, who had a cork leg and wore top boots, was the master. As he had to stretch his cork leg under his table, the boys used to drop a penknife occasionally into it, when he was busily engaged in looking over another boy's work. On one occasion, so Edward Coleridge recalled, a penknife went by mistake into his sound instep, and 'a grand row ensued'.

Between 6 p.m. and 8 p.m. the pupils had to prepare their 'Night Task' (or 'prep.', as it is now called), and so to bed. Such was the long forbidding day in the life of a King's School boy in those times, and he got little or no assistance from books or lexicons. He had to rely upon his initiative, and work things out for himself as best he could, which was often a daunting task for a young boy.

Some outstanding scholars

Brief mention must be made of a few distinguished pupils of the school. Some of them went on to the universities to enter the church, the professions, or the armed forces.

Among the churchmen was John Luxmore, D.D., who became successively Bishop of Bristol, Hereford, and, finally, St Asaph in North Wales. Then there was Richard Hurrell Froude (1803–36) who went on to Eton, and then to Oriel College, Oxford, where he became a fellow. He was a friend of John Henry Newman and, in collaboration with him, contributed eight poems in *Lyra Apostolica* (1836). He wrote three of the *Tracts for the Time*, and supported what came to be known as 'the Oxford Movement'. He was described as 'a man of rare ability'.

George James Cornish (1794–1849) was born at the Manor House, and, after attending the King's School, went to Westminster School, was elected scholar of Corpus Christi College, Oxford, and obtained a first-class in *Literis Humanioribus*. He became a prebendary of Exeter Cathedral.

Of the Coleridge family, several generations were pupils of the school, and were to add lustre by their brilliant achievements. James Duke Coleridge (1789–1857) was the eldest son of Colonel James Coleridge. He took holy orders, and eventually became a prebendary of Exeter Cathedral. His younger brother, John Taylor Coleridge (1790–1876) also received his early education at the King's School before being sent to Eton. At Corpus Christi College, Oxford, he obtained the signal honour of a first class, which included no other name. He was elected a fellow of Exeter College. Called to the bar, he became recorder of Exeter, and in 1835 was appointed a judge of the King's Bench.

Henry Nelson Coleridge (1798–1843) was the fourth son of Colonel Coleridge, and was born at the Chanter's House (then known as Heath's Court). He became a fellow of King's College, Cambridge, and was called to the bar. He married his cousin, Sara Coleridge, in 1828, and later edited the *Literary Remains of Samuel Taylor Coleridge,* who was his uncle and father-in-law. William Hart Coleridge (1789–1849), the only child of Luke Herman Coleridge, who was an elder brother of the poet, went to Christ Church, Oxford, after leaving the King's School, and obtained the unique distinction of a double first in Classics and Mathematics. He was consecrated first Bishop of Barbados and the Leeward Islands. During the last 14 months of his life he was warden of St. Augustine's College, Canterbury, and died suddenly on 21 December 1849. Salston House at Ottery St Mary was built by him as his family home, but is now a residential hotel.

There must be added to these names of notable scholars that of Sir Francis Buller (1746–1800), who came to Ottery St Mary as a pupil of the Rev. John Coleridge on the latter's appointment as master of the King's School. Whilst still a pupil, he was married by special licence at Ottery parish church to Susannah (Susan) Yarde, whose family lived at the Warden's House. He was called to the bar, and made such rapid advancement that he was a Puisne Judge of the King's Bench at the early age of thirty-two.

Later, he came near to being appointed Chief Justice in succession to Lord Mansfield, but instead received 'the very inadequate compensation of a baronetcy'. His only son adopted the additional surname of 'Yarde', and became Yarde-Buller. In 1858, his grandson was made first Baron Churston.

Nineteenth century

During the time that the Rev. George Coleridge was master there had been some 45 boarders at the school, for each of whom fees of 50 guineas (£52.50) a year were charged. These fees helped considerably to augment the headmaster's income.

When George Coleridge retired in 1808, he did so to make way for one of his former pupils, Dr. John Warren, who succeeded him. The number of pupils attending the school during his period as master approached two hundred, and among these were Richard Hurrell Froude, of whom mention has already been made, as well as other noteworthy names. The high standard set by his predecessor was carefully maintained.

There was an amusing incident in October 1819 when three pupils climbed up under the church roof and placed a 'token' coin, wrapped in a piece of paper, under the rafters of the north tower. The paper bore a message offering a reward of £10 to the finder after 1828, provided 'our bones are not rotten by then'. In fact, this cryptic note, and the coin, which was dated 1774, were not discovered until 1967 during an inspection of the church fabric.

The Rev. Sidney William Cornish, D.D., was appointed master of his old school in 1824. He had been educated in part at the King's School, and went on to Exeter College, Oxford, where he gained a second class, and was elected a fellow. After being headmaster of the King's School for 17 years, he also became vicar of Ottery

St Mary. He showed a particular interest in local history, and compiled his *Short Notes on the Church and Parish of Ottery St Mary, Devon,* first published in 1869, which contained much useful information. He was also responsible for compiling a valuable register of the names of pupils of the school between 1795 and 1863, on which latter date he resigned as master. He continued as vicar of the parish until his death in 1873.

After the middle of the 19th century the school faced a rapid decline. There were several reasons for this. Grammar schools were essentially local in character, and the teaching of the classics had been their main object. Those subjects of use in competitive and qualifying examinations were now regarded as being of greater importance than a classical education, and 'proprietory schools' were providing better opportunities. As the King's School, like many other grammar schools, had been founded in the Tudor period, the endowment had become totally inadequate, and it was possible for a good headmaster to earn a much higher salary elsewhere. It was no longer possible to meet the expense of keeping the school in proper repair and, as we shall see in Chapter Ten, the site and buildings eventually had to be sold. But before the close of the century this old school was to make a successful revival in another part of the town.

Chapter Seven

IN STUART TIMES

THE 17th CENTURY spanned one of the most eventful and politically disturbed periods in English history. It began at a time of gathering storm and unrest, which was to lead to the bitterness of civil war and closed with the glorious revolution under William of Orange, and the establishing of democracy.

Churchgoing became a function of social life; one met neighbours there, ogled beauty (in the manner of Samuel Pepys) and observed clothes, besides criticising the sermon. Country people did not travel far from home, for the town or village in which they lived provided for most of their needs. The nobility and gentry had their own coaches, but the poorer folk, when obliged to travel, went by wagon with its attendant discomfort.[1] Riding by post horse, although more costly, provided a quicker means of travel. But the roads were mostly very rough and difficult to traverse, and the traveller was faced with many hazards and dangers.

Cloth-making

Cloth manufacture had become one of the great industries of the country. Early in the Tudor period woollen manufacture had increased considerably with the introduction of kerseys, which were coarse narrow cloths woven from long wool. In 1535 the market had moved from Crediton to Exeter, and this city became the busy centre of a flourishing trade. The white broadcloth was taken by pack-horse to London, where it was dyed and finished.

Dutch, Flemish and other cloth-workers, who had fled from the religious persecution of the ruthless Duke of Alva, settled in Devon and other parts of England, and enriched the trade by bringing to it their skill and their industry. New types of cloth, such as serges and various worsteds, were introduced to capture new markets in Europe.

The South-West became renowned for quality broadcloth, which clothed the gentry and the wealthy merchants. Exeter was famed for its serges, and country folk in the surrounding towns and villages were busily engaged in making medlays, baizes and light cloths for export to Spain, France, Italy and the Levant. Cloth-making was rural in its setting, for it was the spinners and weavers of the country areas who worked for the wealthy woollen merchants of Exeter. Much of this work was part-time, and the country folk were supplied with the wool, which they weaved on the looms in their cottage homes. The spinning was done by women and girls, whilst men worked the looms, but the work was hard and the standard of life for these people was poor. The making of serge was the main source of employment in Ottery St Mary, and was to continue so until the end of the century. But the export trade was seriously affected by political and religious disruption in Central Europe, particularly during the Thirty Years' War (1618–38).

The parish clerk

The office of parish clerk is of great antiquity, and ranked next in dignity to the clergy, although it was of a temporal nature. A layman appointed as parish clerk had to be of good character, competent to read, write, and, if possible, sing.

The earliest parish register at Ottery St Mary is a parchment-book consisting of 250 closely-written pages of entries of baptisms, marriages and burials from the year 1601 to the end of July 1635. The first entries of baptism and burial are dated 2 May 1601, whilst the register of marriages begins on 8 June in that same year.

In 1610 John Vowell was appointed parish clerk, and the church governors agreed that he should occupy the clerk's house for two years at a rent of 40s. (£2.00), and afterwards at the will of the governors and assistants at such rent as they should consider fit, and 'according to his behaviour'. But he did not behave well, for at the end of the two years he was deprived of his office as parish clerk for 'many misdemeanours'.

On 14 February 1613, the governors decided to appoint Thomas Axe, the elder, in his place, and the clerk's house was granted to him on the same terms. The name Axe was common in East Devon and in parts of West Somerset. Thomas Axe's third child, George, was later to become parish clerk during a momentous period in England's history. He was born in January 1608, and was baptized in Ottery church on 7th of that month, for it was then usual for baptisms to take place amidst great rejoicings within a few days of the birth.

One of the clerk's duties was to ring the church bell, and in the minutes of the church corporation for March 1625 it is recorded '. . . that the Clerk do knoll the bell one quarter of an hour before Prayer begins on the week days'.

Later that year Thomas Axe, the elder, appears to have got into serious trouble, and his appointment as parish clerk was in danger. Complaints were made against him for selling drink in his house, which, said the church governors, 'in our opinion deserves present expulsion from his place, but upon his submission and promise of reformation of all his misdemeanours, and for that he hath great charge of children' he was allowed to retain his office, provided there was no further cause for complaint. Regrettably, he had also allowed the clerk's house, for which he had paid no rent for 13 years, to fall into a ruinous condition. He was ordered by the governors to repair this at his own expense. As to the arrears of rent, it was decided that, as he also discharged the duties of organist in the church 'on the Sabbath and on Festival days', he should thenceforth be allowed to live rent free.

By 1634 the duties of parish clerk were being performed by the Rev. Roger Ware, M.A., who had been appointed chaplain priest—but he appears to have been in failing health. By the end of November in that year it would seem that George Axe, the son of Thomas Axe, the elder, was acting as parish clerk.

John Forward had been appointed vicar towards the end of 1625 in succession to his father, the Rev. Nicholas Forward, who had occupied that office for 35 years. Because of his state of health, the Rev. Roger Ware requested the church governors to appoint Hugh Gundrie as chaplain priest in his place, and the bishop's licence was granted for his appointment, but the governors then decided to elect Thomas Forward, the vicar's son. They contended that, because of Roger Ware's indisposition, it was necessary to have two chaplain priests, as originally provided under the royal charter of 1545, so Hugh Gundrie was elected to 'one Chaplain Priest's place'. It was arranged that he should live in the Minister's House of the former collegiate foundation. This appears to be the only occasion on which two chaplain priests were appointed.

Roger Ware died early in 1634/35,[2] and George Axe is described as 'pish Clarke' in the entry of the burial of his first child, Rebecca, on 26 January 1634/35. He had married Judith Churchill, a widow, at Ottery church in October 1633, and their daughter, Rebecca, had died when two months old. The rate of child mortality was high, and a mother could seldom hope to bring up all her children.

Their second child was born on 22 December 1635, and they named him Thomas, after his grandfather. He was baptized at Ottery church five days after his birth. As parish clerk, George Axe recorded the day and hour of his son's birth in the register, although it was not until 1645 that the date of birth was required to be registered in addition to the baptism. However, the day and hour of birth were often entered, so as to assist the astrologer in 'casting a nativity', or telling the future fortune of a child, should this be desired. Thomas Axe was to become a generous benefactor to his birthplace, and his name is perpetuated by the charitable bequests of his will (*see* p. 54).

Although Ottery St Mary was a busy market town, actively engaged in weaving and cloth-making, baking and brewing, farming and milling, there was considerable poverty and disease. In 1635 the church governors paid tailors to make clothes for the poor, and provide sheets, smocks and shoes for the needy. A sum of £4 was spent on sick poor people 'in their great neede and necessity'.

The Civil War in the West

The clouds, which had been rapidly gathering, led to an inevitable clash between king and parliament, and when on 22 August 1642 Charles I raised his standard at Nottingham, the storm broke. The Great Civil War had begun. On all sides there were divided loyalties in a country split by bitterness, and that parliamentarian general, Sir William Waller, expressed the feelings of many families when he wrote, 'That Great God, which is the searcher of my heart, knows with what a sad sense I go upon this service, and with what a perfect hatred I detest this war without an enemy'.

Exeter, regardless of its motto 'Semper Fidelis'—'the Ever Faithful City'—held strong parliamentarian sympathies, and careful preparations were made to withstand the royalist siege, which began on 19 June 1643, and lasted until 4 September, when the city was forced to surrender. Shortly afterwards, Charles I entered in triumph, and Exeter became for a while the headquarters of the royalist army in the West.

The widespread disruption caused during these troublous times was to be reflected in the parish registers. George Axe (1608–79), who was a conscientious parish clerk, felt it very keenly when he was deprived of his office. He revealed his injured feelings in a memorandum written inside the back cover of the register of baptisms, when this was eventually returned to his possession. The birth of his fifth child, George, in August 1643 'was neglected to be Duely Registered in the tyme I was kept out from officiating my place of a pish Clerke in Ottery St Mary'. The entry of the baptism of his son was interpolated in the register.

As Queen Henrietta was expecting a child, Exeter was considered a safe retreat for her and so, on 16 June 1644, she gave birth to Princess Henrietta Anne at Bedford House.[3] But by now the parliamentary troops under the Earl of Essex were approaching Devon, and when news was received that they had reached Axminster, the queen decided to take flight, leaving her four weeks' old daughter in the city.

On 25 July, King Charles arrived at Honiton, and went on to Exeter the next day, where he saw his infant daughter for the first time. He followed the Earl of Essex into Cornwall, and engaged his parliamentary forces at Lostwithiel, inflicting a severe defeat on them.

But by early October 1645, the parliamentarians were approaching Exeter under Sir Thomas Fairfax, who had won a decisive victory over the royalist army at the Battle of Naseby in the previous June. The royalist troops quartered at Ottery St Mary decided to withdraw westwards across the river Exe, for the South-West was still held by the king.

Then on 29 October 1645, Sir Thomas Fairfax 'sent away the train of artillery towards St Mary Autree, and followed after himself'. His army was in need of a rest after the successful campaigns of that summer. He decided to quarter his weary troops at Ottery St Mary, and was entertained at the Chanter's House as the guest of Robert Collins from Saturday, 15 November. Colonel Sir Henry Ireton accompanied him as Commissary, and he also had with him Colonel John Pickering, who had fought at Naseby, been present at the storming of Bridgwater, and had taken a courageous part in the capture of Bristol.

Whilst Fairfax's troops were stationed at Ottery St Mary, he rode over to Broad Clyst and Poltemore to inspect the preparations being made for the attack, which it was planned to launch against Exeter in the coming spring. It was while Fairfax was staying at the Chanter's house that a pleasant ceremony took place in 'The Great Parlour'. Certain members of parliament, in the name of both houses, presented him with 'a fair jewel, set with diamonds of great value which they tied with blue ribbon, and hung about his neck in grateful recognition of his signal services at the Battle of Naseby'.

Also in the Great Parlour of the Chanter's house, a meeting was held between Oliver Cromwell and Sir Thomas Fairfax to decide upon the next stage of the campaign in the West. In his *History of Devonshire,* the Rev. Richard Polwhele stated that Cromwell called upon the people of Ottery St Mary and the surrounding district to raise men and money for the Civil War, but they showed great reluctance to comply with this requisition. A remonstrance was supported by the church governors and leading inhabitants of the parish, and it is believed that Cromwell was so incensed by this refusal that he ordered his soldiers to destroy the stained-glass windows, and any remaining statues or ornaments in the church. He had no respect for such things, as was well shown by the behaviour of his troops in other churches, and the iconoclasts did their destructive work. When the weathercock was taken down during restoration work on the spire of the north tower of Ottery church in 1908/9, it revealed several bullet holes, and had, possibly, provided a target for the roundheads. More recently, a quantity of lead shot has been discovered embedded in the great west doors.

Towards the end of November (1645) there was a recurrence of the bubonic plague, and by 6 December the parliamentary troops were forced to leave the town. John Sprigg recounted in his *England's Recovery* (1845 edn.) that Fairfax was '. . . disposing of the quarters for the foot, who were sick in most places, there dying of soldiers and inhabitants in the town of Autree, seven, eight, and nine a day for several weeks together, insomuch that it was not held safe for the headquarters to be continued there any longer'. Members of the general's family, and half the soldiery of the foot regiments were stricken by this pestilence. Among those who died was Colonel John Pickering, that 'pious active gentleman, who lived so much to God and his Country'. His death was a sad blow to the parliamentarians, and it was decided to move their quarters to Tiverton for the rest of the winter.

The death rate during the early part of 1645 had been less than ten a month, but in November this had risen to 18, and in December to a dramatic total of eighty. During the first 15 days of January 1645/46 a further 37 were buried, and then the entries in the register of burials ceased suddenly, and were not resumed until 8 May in that year. The deaths registered during the plague do not appear to include any of the parliamentarian troops, who were possibly buried outside the town. Tales are told of how a pit was dug in land on the east of the Sidmouth Road, and the bodies of the soldiers, with their clothes on, were thrown into this communal grave. The field was thereafter known as Bury Meadow.

With the arrival of spring in 1646, the parliamentarian army under Sir Thomas Fairfax launched the long-awaited attack upon Exeter, which surrendered after little resistance on 13 April. Meanwhile, the Princess Henrietta, who had remained in the city since her birth, was granted free escort to any part of England her guardian might choose. A few months later she was successfully smuggled across the Channel to France.

William Browne (1588–1645)

William Browne was born at Tavistock in 1588 and was educated at the grammar school there before going on to study at Exeter College, Oxford. He appears to have been more interested in devoting himself to the muses, and found patrons in the earls of Pembroke.

He wrote *The Shepherd's Pipe,* but is best remembered for his narrative poem *Britannia's Pastorals,* descriptive of the beautiful Devon countryside. His poetry sprang largely from his native soil, and shows a genuine love of nature.

> My music for lofty pitches shall not roam,
> But homely pipen of my native home.

It is thought that his poetry influenced Milton, Keats, and Elizabeth Barrett Browning. He is known to have spent his last years at Ottery St Mary, and the epitaphs to members of the Sherman family in the parish church are attributed to him (*see* Chapter Eleven, p. 96).

Because of his association with Devon, and his poetic descriptions of the surrounding countryside, he was much admired by Samuel Taylor Coleridge, who even went so far as to claim that the Coleridges were 'connected' with his family.[4]

The parish register contains an entry that 'William Browne' was buried at Ottery St Mary on 1 December 1645 and, as there is no mention of the author of *Britannia's Pastorals* after that date or any trace of him having died elsewhere, it is believed that this entry relates to him. If so, then it seems likely that he was an early victim of the bubonic plague.

George Axe becomes 'Parish Register'

After George Axe was deprived of his office as parish clerk in 1643, the registers were kept very indifferently for the next two years, and towards the end of 1645 the entries ceased altogether. They were not resumed until May 1648, when George Axe triumphantly proclaimed at the top of the page in the register of baptisms:

> Christenings since the eighth day of May 1648 on which day by an unanimous consent of the pishioners in the pish Church of Ottery Ste. Mary I, George Axe, was Re-established to be their pish Clarke as formerly I was.

Then on Sunday, 30 January 1649, King Charles was beheaded in Whitehall and a wave of horror and dismay swept through the whole nation when the news became known. As one who witnessed the king's execution was later to explain, 'there came from the crowd such a groan as I never heard before and desire I may never hear again'.

By an Act of Parliament passed on 24 August 1653 (Praise God Barebones' Parliament), the clergy were required to give up their registers to laymen, duly elected as 'parish Registers', and marriages were thenceforth to be solemnised by a civil magistrate and not by the clergy. It was fortunate that the continuity of George Axe's duties was preserved when, on 19 September 1653, he was elected and chosen to be register for the parish of Ottery St Mary. Two days later he was sworn before a magistrate 'truly to pforme the duty of a pish Register there according to the Tenor of the said Act'.

After 29 September 1653 no marriage was to be celebrated without the register's certificate that he had published banns on three 'successive Lord's Days at the close of the Morning Exercise in the public meeting place, commonly called the Church, or Chapel, or (if the parties preferred it) in the nearest market-place on three successive market days'.

George Axe, as 'parish register', was required to enter in the registers in his keeping all publications of banns, which he did under the heading of 'Publications of Purposes of Marriages Received Published and Registered . . .'. Details of the banns of marriage were carefully kept from 1653 until 1657, and were set out more fully than the actual entry of marriage; for example, the occupations of the parties were usually stated.

The experiment of civil registration was successful, for the register books from 1653 to 1660 were kept exceptionally well. George Axe made the entries with considerable care and detail, and was as scrupulous in carrying out his duties as 'parish register' as he had been as parish clerk. The vicar resumed officiating at marriages after 20 November 1657, although the entries of the 'Purposes of Marriage' continued until 13 May 1660.

The varied occupations and descriptions in the register books are of considerable interest, and throw valuable light on the social history of those times. A glance at the register of burials during the Stuart period shows that many of the inhabitants were engaged in the cloth trade. We find such descriptions as 'weaver', 'ffuller' (one who cleansed and thickened cloth), 'woollcomer' or 'worstercomber' (one who combed wool, to prepare it for spinning) and 'clothyer'. George Axe's stepson, William Churchill, was described as a 'searge weaver'.

Among other trades mentioned are many which have long since fallen into disuse. There are such varied descriptions as blacksmith, cooper (a maker of casks), 'cordwyner' (cordwainer, a shoemaker), 'cureargeon' (surgeon), 'ffelmonger' (a dealer in animal hides and skins), 'hatter', 'husbandman' (a farmer), 'maulster' (a maker of malt), 'mercer' (a dealer in rich textiles, especially silks), 'scrivener' (a drafter of documents, a writer), 'sope-boyler', 'tanner' (a maker of leather from raw hides), 'trumpetter', and 'whitebaker' (a maker of white bread). Other interesting descriptions in the registers at this time are 'an old almes mayde', 'an old man and oastler at the White Hart', 'an auncient housekeeper' (male), 'a maide childe unbaptized', 'a poore man of ye town', and 'one of the ffour Gouvenors of this Corporation'. Other occupations are 'yeoman' (a small farmer), 'taylor' (tailor), 'saylor', 'a souldier', 'an old workeman', and 'ye old bedman' (the name by which the sexton was known until late Victorian times). The erratic spelling of George Axe possesses its own particular charm.

'. . . the King enjoys his own again'

Before entering marriages in the parish register following the Restoration of Charles II, George Axe expressed his delight by heading the new page in his bold handwriting:

> The Nyne and twentyeth day of Maye in ye year 1660, being ye Joyfull Day of his Majs Coming into England, from henceforth I Register ye Marriages onely according to ye Auncient Custom.

Similar entries were made in the registers of other parishes expressing the joy of the Restoration.

The parishioners of Ottery St Mary paid a total of £190 13s. 1d. (£190.66) for the disbandment of the Cromwellian army. A list of the sums paid is preserved among the documents belonging to Ottery church corporation. Gideon Haydon of Cadhay was required to pay £10, which was a fairly large sum in those days, and his widowed mother, Margaret Haydon, had to pay £3 6s. 8d. (£3.33).

Early in December 1660 the Rev. John Forward died after having been vicar for nearly 35 years. He was succeeded in March 1661 by the Rev. Melchizedeck Alford, who was a member of an ardent royalist family found throughout the West Country. The Civil War had interrupted his student days at Christ Church, Oxford. He was a notable cavalier and had become treasurer to the royal garrison at Exeter, when it was besieged by the parliamentarians in 1646. He had conveyed letters to Charles I at Oxford and elsewhere, and assisted in carrying off the Duke of Gloucester to safety. However, he was overlooked on the Restoration, and was never rewarded for his services. He died early in August 1689 'possessed of no greater preferment than the Poor Vicaridge of Autrey in Devon'. His wife, Elizabeth, survived him for some years, and did much for the care of the sick and elderly in the town, as will be mentioned later.

Protestant dissenters

The Great Civil War had caused bitter rivalries between families, which had torn the country apart. The Haydons of Cadhay were ardent royalists, and Nicholas Haydon had in 1649 been fined the sum of £69 4s. 6d. (£69.225) 'for delinquency in adhering to the forces raised against Parliament'. But Robert Collins of the Chanter's House had parliamentarian sympathies, and his father had entertained Fairfax when he made his headquarters at Ottery St Mary in 1645. A bitter enmity grew up between the two families.

Robert Collins took holy orders, and was appointed vicar of Talaton, but this was to augur ill for him. A previous incumbent, Mr. Pynsent, had been removed from the living as being 'a scandalous minister', but he continued to reside in the parish vowing that he would not enter the church again until he was reinstated as vicar. On the Restoration of Charles II he was, in fact, restored to the benefice. The Act of Uniformity of 1662 required clergymen to declare their 'unfeigned consent and assent' to everything contained in the book of common prayer, but the Rev. Robert Collins refused to do this. He had, in consequence, been deprived of his benefice and was regarded as a nonconformist. In all, some 2,000 clergy, who would not accept the restored prayer book, were turned adrift without compensation.

The religious upheaval of the times is reflected in the parish registers. An entry dated 18 August 1663 records that 'Symon ye son of Mr. Robert Collins' was buried 'without Common Prayer', and later that year we find that 'Nathaniell, ye son of Richard Cheeke, was buried without a Minister or service'.

The Conventicle Act of 1664 made it a criminal offence if more than five persons, other than members of the same household, met for any act of dissenting worship. The penalty was a fine or imprisonment for the first and second offences, and transportation for seven years for the third offence. On information being received that a prayer meeting had taken place at the Chanter's House, a warrant was issued to break open the doors and seize Robert Collins and others, and on 25 September 1670 the churchwardens and constables, followed by a great mob, marched to his house and arrested him. He was brought before the local magistrate, Sir Peter Prideaux of Netherton Hall, Farway, who told him that he was a minister of the devil, and fined him the sum of forty pounds. An appeal to Quarter Sessions was to no avail. As there had been no sermon at the parish church on Sunday, 20 August 1675, Robert Collins decided to preach to a large gathering of neighbours and other sympathisers in his own house, and as a result he suffered a further fine. In 1678 he was sent to prison for a similar offence.

At the Manor House lived Warwick Ledgingham, who was lord of the manor of Ottery. As a near neighbour of Robert Collins, he must have been aware of these unlawful religious meetings, but he failed to report them. He was convicted for this and fined £10.

On 20 August 1679 Nicholas Haydon, who viewed the Collins family with intense dislike, led a mob to the Chanter's House and broke down the gates and doors. However, his search was foiled, but it was later learned that 23 people had been assembled there for a prayer meeting, but had quickly dispersed. They were convicted at the Quarter Sessions of being an unlawful assembly, and Robert Collins was again sent to prison.

After these happenings, a close watch must have been kept on the Chanter's House, for another raid was made on 15 May 1681 by Nicholas Haydon, accompanied by constables. On being refused admission, they broke open 'the great gate, and then the doors', but, on this occasion, only three persons were found, other than the family, the others having made their escape.

However, 10 days later Robert Collins was riding to Talaton to attend a funeral, when he was stopped by Gideon Haydon of Cadhay and was requested to take the corporation oath, which required him to take holy communion according to the rites of the Church of England. This he refused to do and was committed to prison for six months at Exeter, where he preached to other prisoners, many of whom, like himself, were dissenters. The persecution continued and Robert Collins was fined £20 for not attending church, and then prosecuted for failing to have his three children baptized. Further penalties were imposed for not receiving holy communion, and for residing within five miles of his former parish of Talaton, contrary to the Five Mile Act 1665. Finally, he was excommunicated, which made it unlawful for him to attend any church services.

He had put up a great fight for religious freedom, but he was now broken in health, and could endure this relentless persecution no longer, so he decided to leave Ottery St Mary. In 1685 he sold the Chanter's House, and went with his family to Holland, where he was at last able to find religious freedom, although he was a shattered man of only 52 years of age.

Five years later he returned to Ottery St Mary, where he spent his last days. He died on 6 March 1698, and by his will he bequeathed the sum of £20 'for the best advantage of the Presbyterian Meeting at Ottery St Mary where I first drew breath'. He had prepared the way for the first 'Church of Christ of Protestant Dissenters' in the town, and this remains one of the earliest nonconformist churches in the country. It is now the United Reformed Church.

Meanwhile, George Axe had continued to serve as parish clerk until his death on 17 July 1679 'about Two of the clock in ye morning'. Except for a short interval during the Civil War, he had been parish clerk of Ottery St Mary for nearly 45 years. He was succeeded in this ancient office by William Ledgingham, whose family lived at the Manor House. On 3 August 1679 Ledgingham was nominated and elected by the vicar and the four governors to be parish clerk 'for so long as he should well behave himself in the said place'.

What's in a Name?

We have seen in an earlier chapter how Ottery St Mary got its name. It was variously shown in ancient documents as Otrig (1061), Otri, Otrei (1086), Oteri (1238), and Otery Sancte Marie (1242). Early map-makers spelt the place-name in a variety of ways. Christopher Saxton, whose *Atlas of England and Wales* (1579) was the first national atlas to be produced in any country, shows it as 'Autre'. The Restoration period was the time of the great county map-makers, and John Ogilby (1600–76) shows it as 'Autrey', while Robert Morden in his county map of 1695 refers to it as 'Autree MARY OTERY' (*see* Fig. 7 opposite).

Monmouth's rebellion

Among the most memorable events in the history of the West Country is the rebellion of James, Duke of Monmouth, and its tragic aftermath. Monmouth, the bastard son of Charles II and Lucy Walter, was the pampered and spoilt darling of a dissolute court, and much doted upon by his father. In 1662, Samuel Pepys (1633–1703) had prophetically recorded in his famous *Diary*:

> The Duke of Monmouth is in so great splendour at Court and so dandled by the King that some doubt, if the King should have no child by the Queen (which there is yet no appearance of), whether he would not be acknowledged for a lawful son, and that there will be a difference follow upon it between the Duke of York and him; which God prevent!

In the late summer of 1680 Monmouth made a triumphant 'progress' in the West Country as far as Exeter. When on this journey, he was entertained by Sir Walter Yonge at the Great House, Colyton, and then went on to Otterton, where he stayed a night with Richard Duke, a member of a worthy local family.

As Monmouth approached Exeter on 1 September, he was met by a party of 'brave stout young men in linen waistcoats and drawers, white and harmless, without so much as a stick in their hands but joining hands'. He stayed a night at the deanery in the 'ever faithful' city, but many of the clergy, and also the civic authorities, held back. The next day he travelled to Honiton along that straight Roman road, passing by Fairmile to the north of Ottery St Mary, and made his return towards London.

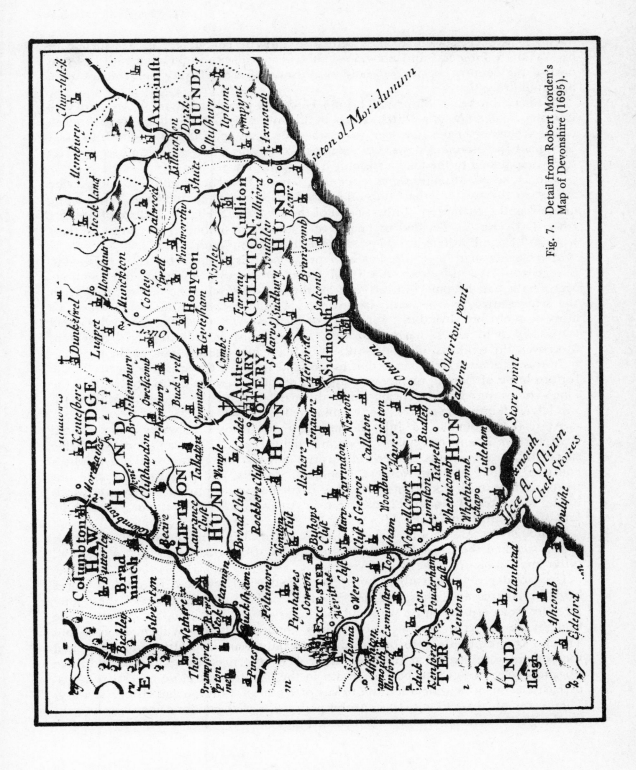

Fig. 7. Detail from Robert Morden's Map of Devonshire (1695).

Nearly five years were to pass before Monmouth, encouraged by the success of his 'Western Progress' and convinced that he could expect loyal support in that part of the country, decided to land in Dorset with a rebel army, and embark upon his fateful rebellion.

As dawn broke on Sunday, 11 June 1685, the people of Lyme Regis awoke to find the *Helderenberg,* a Dutch frigate of 32 guns, supported by three small tenders, riding at anchor in the bay. The town was soon astir, and the mayor set off in haste to spread the alarming news. On reaching Exeter, he arranged for an urgent letter to be despatched to the king informing him of this insurrection.

The Duke of Monmouth, attended by about 80 officers and 150 men, came ashore to the west of the Cobb and raised his standard of rebellion, proclaiming himself as the champion of liberty and of the Protestant religion. Instead of heading towards Exeter, he decided to march to Taunton, described as 'the most factious town in England', where he was proclaimed 'King Monmouth'.

After being sharply rebuffed as he approached Bristol, his rebel army engaged in a successful skirmish with the royal forces at Norton St Philip. But by now, Monmouth had become disheartened by the lack of support he had received from the Whig gentry, the powerful landowners of the South-West, added to which his army was already dwindling, for many of his men were deserting. The gentry had cautiously held aloof, having no wish to take part in this ill-judged rebellion. Moreover, the weakness of Monmouth's title made him unacceptable to them.

It was with some reluctance that he decided to move towards Bridgwater in the forlorn hope of gaining further recruits. He reached there on 2 July to find that the king's forces were by now encamped on the marshy waste of Sedgemoor. Monmouth was left with only one course open to him: he must fight.

At dusk on Sunday, 5 July, he marched out from Bridgwater along the old Bristol road intent on making a daring night attack. This came near to being successful, but once the element of surprise was lost, his ill-equipped army, which consisted mainly of farm-workers, labourers, weavers, and peasants, was soon put to rout. Monmouth fled from the field of battle but was captured shortly afterwards hiding in a ditch at Horton Plantation, near Ringwood. A week later he suffered the fate of all traitors on Tower Hill.

Although the Monmouth Rebellion took place mainly in Dorset and Somerset, it also touched the fringe of East Devon, and its aftermath was to leave a deep and bitter impression upon that countryside.

On Monday, 14 September, Lord Chief Justice Jeffreys and four other judges held the Assizes at Exeter, and sentenced to death 21 prisoners, but of these only 12 were executed. Of those who had taken part in the rebellion, about forty were brought up for trial. Among those rebels condemned were William Parsons and Thomas Quintin, who were both ordered to be executed at Ottery St Mary, and four others were hanged at Honiton. Some were sentenced to be flogged and these floggings were ordered to be carried out in the 'greater and more general markets' of East Devon, which included the towns of Honiton, Colyton and Ottery St Mary. The horror of 'the Duking Days', as this period after Sedgemoor came to be known, was long to be remembered. It was recorded that

The great oaks of village greens had their ghastly loads, the steeples of quiet country churches were decorated with gory heads, and even the direction posts at corners of roads were transformed into gibbets—and for years after. The dark memories of that cruel time still live in the Western counties.

The Glorious Revolution

Over three years were to pass before William, Prince of Orange, driven by a 'Protestant Wind', sailed into Torbay with a Dutch fleet, and landed at Brixham. He had come over from Holland in response to an invitation to invade England and safeguard the Protestant faith, and to protect his wife's hereditary rights to the Crown.

On 9 November 1688, with his motley army he entered Exeter by the west gate, and set up his headquarters at the deanery, the dean having already fled in panic. It was here that Prince William decided to await the promised support of the country gentry of the South-West. But, with the dreadful retribution meted out to those who had rallied to Monmouth's standard still fresh in their minds, they at first held back. However, after initial hesitation, the powerful landowners gradually came forward to offer William their support as the champion of Protestant liberty. So far as the theory of hereditary succession was concerned, William was married to James II's eldest daughter, Mary, and he himself was a lawful nephew of the king, and a grandson of Charles I.

Among the first of those influential landowners to join him was Sir William Portman, bart., of Orchard, near Taunton in Somerset who, accompanied by his steward, Thomas Axe, eldest son of Ottery's notable parish clerk, hastened to Exeter, and other members of the country gentry soon followed. Meanwhile, advance units of Prince William's army were already stationed at the market towns of Ottery St Mary and Honiton.

By now William was sufficiently encouraged to set out from Exeter and make cautious progress eastwards towards London. It may have been at the suggestion of Thomas Axe that he called at Ottery St Mary on 21 November, when on his way to Axminster, for he was accompanied by Sir William Portman and his steward, among other supporters. He dined at the little town and, on reaching Axminster without opposition, decided to remain there for four days to reorganise his army. Then, by gradual stages, William approached London, and on 18 December he entered the capital amidst great rejoicings.

Five days later, James II conveniently fled to France, and into exile: the reign of the last Stuart king was over. William of Orange and his wife, the Princess Mary, were crowned in Westminster Abbey on 11 April 1689, which was the only double coronation in English history, Mary being crowned as Queen Regnant. The long and bitter struggle between Crown and parliament, which the Civil War had failed to resolve, had eventually been settled by a bloodless revolution, and the sovereignty of parliament was established.

William had been anxious to secure for the Dutch the support of England against his implacable enemy Louis XIV of France. On 26 May 1690 a rate was made to raise money towards 'the Reducing of Ireland and prosecuting the Warre agst

France'. The poll for Ottery St Mary showed a population of 1,632 at that time, and it is interesting to note that of the names recorded there was only one with more than one christian name. The assessment for the town amounted to £128 12s. 8d. (£128.63).

Thomas Axe: an Ottery benefactor

On entering the south porch of the parish church a large stone tablet on the west wall records certain charitable bequests made by Thomas Axe. His interesting will is dated 20 July 1691.

The nature of these bequests, the careful division into special funds, and the emphasis on encouraging 'Steadiness, Sobriety and Industry' never fails to arouse the curiosity of the many visitors to the church. Their interest is increased when they are assured that the trusts of the will are still administered by the church governors, who were nominated by this judicious benefactor as trustees for this purpose.

Thomas Axe attended the King's School under John Ball, M.A., who was the master from 1636 until 1651, and married Dorothy Birstall, the daughter of William Birstall, M.A., who succeeded John Ball as master, having been formerly school-master at Blandford in Dorset. He obtained employment under Mr. Colby, the steward of the estates of Sir William Portman. The Portmans were an old family of Somerset squires, and had recently bought a country estate at Bryanston, near Blandford, and were proposing to build a fine mansion-house overlooking the leisurely flowing river Stour, and to lay out elaborate formal gardens. It was, no doubt, largely through his father-in-law that Thomas Axe was successful in obtaining the position as assistant to the steward.

He appears to have been well liked by Sir William Portman and his family, some of whom were godparents to his children, and they left to him certain property at Blandford and Southwark. He succeeded Mr. Colby as steward to Sir William, and died at Orchard Portman in July 1691 at the age of fifty-five. He was a local boy, who by his industry and steadfast efforts had made good, and he was ever mindful of his birthplace.

Under his will he established a generous charity in which he showed considerable foresight. He directed that three-twelfths of the profits of his Blandford property should be applied

> To some man or woman or exemplary life & some Skill in Physick & Surgery who should industriously endeavour to help all the poor of Ottery gratis in cases of Sickness and Accident till better advice could be had,

and thereby founded an early first-aid service. He expressed the wish that the vicar's wife for the time being should be preferred before all others for these duties, if she should 'be very fitt or as fitt as Mrs. Alford, the late Vicar's wife, who delighted in such things'. He went on to explain that 'the skill is learnt in a month or two'. Mrs. Elizabeth Alford was the widow of the Rev. Melchizedeck Alford (*see* p. 48), and Thomas Axe appears to have held a high opinion of her as 'a doctress (as they call them)' administering to the sick and needy.

He directed that part of the income of his houses in Southwark should be set aside as a fund to provide marriage portions to any young man or woman who had served in one employment in the parish of Ottery St Mary for seven years, and had not received alms within five years of marriage. The present payments are £40 on marriage, followed by £20 on each of the next three anniversaries, with a final payment of £50 on the fifth anniversary of the marriage. The qualifying period of employment is no longer required, but it is a condition that the applicant must have resided in Ottery St Mary or the immediate locality for at least five years, and be aged 21 or over at the time of the marriage.

A distribution of income was also directed to be made about St Thomas's Day (21 December) among 'Elderly and Sober Housekeepers who have lived well and not received alms of the Parish within five years' none to have less than £1 'the less they need it the better they will be able to give an Alms to such as are in want'. The description 'housekeeper', in this sense, meant a man or woman who owned their house and were, therefore, better able to help others in a less fortunate position in life.

A further part of the Southwark rents was to be used to create a fund out of which 'to lend to such poore men to supply their stocks as have not had alms of the parish for five years back and are industrious and sober'. Preference was to be given to his next-of-kin; next, to those born in the parish of Ottery St Mary; then, those engaged in husbandry; next, those employed in linen or woollen manufacture; then, artificers and handicraftsmen, and, lastly, shopkeepers.

The vicar, the minister, the grammar schoolmaster, and the parish clerk were not overlooked, for the will provided for a share of the income of Thomas Axe's property to be made to each of them.

On becoming steward of the Portman estates, Thomas Axe had moved to Orchard, near Taunton, which was the principal seat of the Portman family. He was buried beneath the shadow of the Blackdown Hills among the apple orchards of a smiling countryside. In the peaceful 'God's Acre' of St Michael's church at Orchard, he was laid to rest on 1 August 1691, but 'never marked the marble with his name'.

The cloth trade

By 1680 the principal market for Devonshire cloth was Holland, but there was a considerable trade with Portugal, Spain and Italy. Topsham was the main port for this great export trade, and by the end of the century the canal was being improved and widened so as to enable larger ships to reach Exeter. Certain merchants, who were engaged in the trade with Holland, were influenced by the Dutch style of architecture when building their houses, as may be seen in The Strand at Topsham.

At this time upwards of £50,000 worth of woollen goods were being sold in Exeter every week and, it is believed, over three-quarters of the population of the city was then engaged in the trade.

On visiting Exeter in 1698, the intrepid Celia Fiennes (1662–1741), who travelled the country on horseback, wrote:

. . . a vast trade is carried on . . . there is an incredible quantity of serges made and sold in the town. The whole town and country is employed for at least twenty miles around in spinning, weaving, dressing and scouring, fulling and drying of the serges. It turns the most money in a week of anything in England. One week with another, there is £10,000 paid in ready money, sometimes £15,000 . . .

Towards the end of Queen Anne's reign, Daniel Defoe (1660–1731), the author of *Robinson Crusoe, Moll Flanders,* and other works, also travelled around Devon recording his impressions, and was much impressed by the industry of the Devonshire people. As he came down Honiton Hill he was ecstatic on beholding the expanse of country stretching away towards the west across the Otter valley, and thought it 'the most beautiful landscape in the World . . . and I do not remember the like in any one place in England'.

Chapter Eight

THE GEORGIAN TOWN

Some houses

IN THE NEIGHBOURHOOD of the church there are some gracious examples of early Georgian architecture, reminders of a more spacious and leisured age. Near the foot of Church Hill (now known as Silver Street) is No. 13, 'Georgian House', an attractive small property with an adjoining antiques shop.

Then, as we proceed up the hill, there stands what is now Barclays Bank, which was once a chemist's shop with large glass bottles, containing coloured liquids, displayed in its windows. Above the first floor windows are ornate mouldings, which were a feature of the Georgian period. A parapet serves to conceal the sloping slate roof.

Beyond the bank is The Lodge, a characteristic town-house of the same period. The narrow curved fascia over the bow window may once have displayed the name of 'Charles D. Mayne', who carried on the business of a bookseller and stationer there during the middle of the 19th century. Steps lead up from the steeply sloping street to the front door, and on the left of this is an iron ring formerly used for tethering horses. The attractive old street lamp fixed to the front of the house recalls nostalgic memories of the days when our streets were lit by gas.

Among architectural features of the house, the raised keystones above the windows should be observed, and at each end of the front are alternate long and short corner stones. Sash windows became popular early in the 18th century, and continued as the standard domestic window until the end of the next century.

Along Cornhill, on the east side of the church, is Stafford House, built about 1760, which is probably so named after Henry, Lord Stafford, Earl of Wiltshire. He was the second husband of Cicely, Marchioness of Dorset, who was responsible for the beautiful Dorset aisle in the church. Cornhill House, which is possibly of slightly earlier date, stands a little higher up the hill.

The Priory was built in 1719, and has been carefully restored in recent years. The front door is approached by a flight of stone steps, and the simple canopy is supported upon ornate brackets. Most houses had up to this date been thatched, so it was something of a novelty when roof drains were introduced. The early rainwater heads were large and made of lead with elaborate ornamentation, which usually displayed the year that the house was built. They were to become 'a status symbol', and those at The Priory clearly show the year as '1719', and are particularly fine examples.

Cornhill formerly continued to the top of the hill, where Paternoster Row originally began, and there were houses on both sides of the road. Along the east side of the churchyard, opposite the entrance (Lambs Court) leading to the hospital, was a row of six cottages. As they had become very dilapidated, they were pulled down about 1869, and their site was added to the churchyard. The three steps which led up to them still remain on the corner.

Beyond these cottages there once stood The Great House, of which little is known, but it appears to have been owned eventually by the Saville family. In *The Story of a Devonshire House* (published in 1905), Lord Coleridge wrote: 'Rock House [now called 'Sandrock'] was formed out of the stables attached to the Great House, which was pulled down at the close of the eighteenth century'.

The site was afterwards used as a private garden. At one time it was known as 'Miss Lee's Garden'—her father lived opposite at The Priory. There were fish ponds in this garden, which were fed by the stream or runlet that comes down from Ridgeway, and continues as an open gully along The College. It appears to have been known as Dabbs Brook.

Hereabouts are several pleasant smaller houses of the Georgian period, which merit careful study, for they possess some interesting features. As we continue round the corner into Paternoster Row some charming houses here date back to the reign of Queen Anne. Their gracious character has been carefully preserved.

There are several Georgian houses in Mill Street. Raleigh House stands on part of the site of an earlier building, which is reputed to have been a residence of that famous Elizabethan courtier, Sir Walter Raleigh. It is known that, after an absence from his native county, he wished to return to Devon, and tried to purchase his birthplace, Hayes Barton, near East Budleigh, but was unsuccessful. An 18th-century historian of Devon, Richard Polwhele, writing of Ottery St Mary in 1793, referred to the mouldering structure in which he stated Sir Walter Raleigh once lived, and described the house as having 'altogether a monasterial appearance'.

The original house was the largest of a block of five which stood out among the adjoining properties in this part of Mill Street. It had stone mullioned windows, and a projecting open porch, with a room above, surmounted by a battlemented parapet. Within the porch were wooden benches on either side. On 15 May 1805, this historic property was destroyed by fire.

Nearby are Colby House, and The Donnithornes, with its walled garden leading down to the Mill Stream. They are good examples of Georgian town houses. Most of the cottages in Mill Street were thatched and built of cob, and several of these on the south side of the street were set back against the steeply rising bank, and approached by steps, which led up to their doors.

William Culne

'All this in every part was done by me Wm. Culne, born in this Parish': these words appear on the carved wooden pulpit in the church.

William Culne was a local craftsman, and made this pulpit in 1722. It displays some beautiful wood carving with the figures of the evangelists in the four panels, and originally stood at the east entrance to the nave. It had an ornate canopy and sounding board above, which was surmounted by a gilded trumpeting angel. This figure was removed, together with the sounding board, during restoration work in 1849–50, and lay discarded for many years before being placed above Bishop Grandisson's ancient clock, which it now adorns in the south transept.

An interesting drawing 'from Nature and on Stone' of the interior of the church looking towards the altar was made by William Spreat of Exeter in 1842. The pulpit, as it was originally, is on the right of this print (*see* Plate 20).

It is believed that William Culne later visited several European countries, where he saw many fine examples of the woodcarvers' skill. He became dissatisfied with his own humble efforts, and it is said that, on his return, he offered to replace his pulpit with one of better and more skilled workmanship. But the parishioners declined his offer, being well pleased with the one he had already made for them.

This pulpit has been greatly treasured, for it displays delightful local craftsmanship, the ears of corn and the scallop shell being beautifully carved. There is no existing record of any earlier pulpit in Ottery church but, as lengthy sermons had been the fashion during the previous century, there would undoubtedly have been one. Under a decree of 1603 every church had to be provided with a 'comely and decent' pulpit.

As this had been a collegiate church prior to the Dissolution, the pulpitum or stone screen at the western end of the chancel was most likely used for this purpose. Sermons may have been preached from the gallery above this screen.

The parish workhouse

In 1738 a parish workhouse, large enough to contain 200 poor persons, was built near St Saviour's bridge. It was a distressing place, for little compassion was shown to the unfortunate inmates in those days. Those who were mentally afflicted were kept chained in the ground-floor rooms, and eagerly seized and devoured the bones and scraps tossed to them through the open windows by passers-by.

When a Union workhouse was opened at Honiton in 1838, the parish workhouse at Ottery St Mary was closed, and no trace remains today.

Corn riots

The failure of the harvest in 1766 caused a considerable increase in the price of bread, and this resulted in some serious rioting at Ottery St Mary. Sir George Yonge, who was a local magistrate, met with great difficulty when he attempted to quell these riots. Corn was forcibly seized from several farms in the neighbourhood, and taken to the market for selling at 5s. 0d. (25p) a bushel, and a flour mill in the town was completely destroyed.

When the magistrate attempted to have a proclamation made in the Flexton, the enraged mob intimidated the town crier to such an extent that he was unable to carry out his duty. Eventually, it was agreed that the price of corn should be fixed at 4s. 9d. (23p) next market day, whereupon Sir George Yonge rode into the town and told the unruly crowds that the military would be called in unless the rioting ceased. He directed that the 'principal inhabitants' should call a meeting, and impress upon the people of the town the fatal consequences which might result if they persisted with their disorderly behaviour.

Manorial courts

In 1761 Edward Norse is shown as being lord of the manor of Ottery. Attaching to the manor were two courts of private jurisdiction, and the tenants had to attend their 'hall-moot'.

The court-leet had criminal jurisdiction, and was in theory presided over by the lord of the manor, but more usually by the steward of the leet acting in his judicial capacity. He had power to impose fines and imprisonment for contempt, and to take recognizances for the peace. The proceedings and decisions of the court were enrolled as a lasting record, and the earliest court rolls still in existence for the manor of Ottery begin in 1378–9. The court-leet had power to punish for all minor offences committed within the jurisdiction of the manor by the tenants and other persons residing there.

The other court was called the court-baron and it was here that the civil business was conducted, such as small claims, and disputes between tenants concerning lands held of the manor. Certain officers were appointed by this court 'for the year Ensueing and until he shall be thereof Lawfully discharged'. Among these were the petty (pettit) constables, for the preservation of good order and behaviour; an inspector of weights and measures; two breadweighers, and an ale-taster, whose duty it was to check the quality and weight of essential food, such as bread and ale. In addition, a water-bailiff, a pig-driver, and a scavenger were also appointed annually.

The court-leet and the court-baron were usually held together, and on these important days in the life of the town the lord's tenants assembled at the ancient manor-hall to the north of the church (*see* Chapter Eleven).

Penalties were also imposed by these courts for encroachments on commons and roads, and on failure to repair fences, ditches, roads and bridges. If we turn to the court rolls of the manor and hundred of Ottery St Mary, we find such entries as:

30 September 1736: The Jury on their Oaths did present as followeth:

That the Bridge over Dabbs-Brook in the footpath leading from Great Well, Ware and other parts to the Church and Market of Ottery St Mary is much out of repair to the great prejudice of His Majesty's Subjects haveing Occasion to Travel that way Which the said Jurors Apprehended ought to be repair'd by Charles Vaughan, Esqr. Ordered that he should repair the same in one month then next under the penalty of Twenty Shillings [£1].

Also That the Water-Bailiff hath neglected to keep the Gutters cleaned up for the passage of the Water through the Town. Ordered that he do keep the said Gutters cleaned up under the penalty of 6s. 8d. [33p] Assessed to 3s. 4d. [17p] (by the Assessors in that behalf duly sworn).

21 April 1768: Jurors returned to enquire as well for our Sovereign Lord the King as the Lord of this Leet:

We present a plott of Ground, which is taken out of the Waste belonging to the Lord of the Manor lying at the higher end of Pigs Street, otherwise Sandhill Street, which Joseph Bradboard, the Younger, made an incroachment upon, being about Thirty feet in length and seven feet in Breadth.

The instruments of punishment, such as the stocks and whipping post, the ducking stool and the pillory were frequently ordered by the court to be kept in good order and repair. On 30 September 1736 it was recorded that 'the Lord of this Manor hath not repaired the Ducking-Stool within the said Manor pursuant to the Order of the former Court'.

The abatement of nuisances could also be ordered by the manorial courts:

21 April 1768: the Jury presented that 'A pump in Flexton or Market place, and likewise a pump in Jesu Street otherwise Yonder Street, being very much out of repair, dangerous of children falling in, as a great Nuisance'.

And 23 October 1761: 'We present Benjamin Leat for keeping Swine in a House Adjoining to the Street, which is a great Nuisance to the publick And therefore We order that the said Benjamin Leat do remove and discontinue the same within Ten days from the date hereof Under the penalty of 6s. 8d. for every week he shall continue the same after that time'.

Also on 5 April 1769: it was presented 'That a Mantle Chimney in the dwellinghouse of Saml. Vinecombe in the Town of Ottery St Mary is very much in decay and dangerous of fireing the Town. Ordered that the said Saml. Vinecombe do Cause the same to be put in good repair or rather rebuilt with Brick in one Month under the penalty of Twenty Shillings'.

The stocks

On the site now occupied by Queen Victoria's Diamond Jubilee Monument at the top of Church Hill (Silver Street) were the town stocks, for it was usual for these to be associated with the market place or, in some cases, with the village green.

Stocks appear to have been in use in England from Saxon times, but it was not until after the Black Death of 1348–49 that every town was required to have them. In Richard II's reign (1377–99) edicts directed that they should be properly maintained in good order and repair.

An Act passed in 1496 stipulated 'that vagabonds, idle and suspected persons, shall be set in the stocks three days and three nights, and have none other sustenance than bread and·water, and then shall be put out of the town. And whosoever shall give such idle person more shall forfeit 12 pence'. The stocks were mostly used in cases of drunkenness, or as an alternative to prison, or on failure to pay a fine for that offence. A similar penalty was later ordered for those who traded on Sunday. Those found tippling and gaming during the hours of divine service could be summarily put in the stocks for varying periods of hours.

The wretched offender was held in ignominious confinement, seated on a low board, or even on the ground, with his ankles firmly secured by being clamped between two planks and, in this uncomfortable position, he was subjected to the ridicule of passers-by, and the abuse of those attending the markets and fairs. With the passing years ideas on penal methods changed gradually, and from early in the 19th century it became less and less usual to subject offenders to public ridicule as a form of punishment. An old Ottery resident could recall that about 1863, when he and other little 'tackers' were coming from school, they 'saw a man in the stocks, watched by a policeman'.

The last occasion on which stocks were used in this country was at Newbury in 1872, when Mark Turk was put in them for being drunk in church. But the punishment of the stocks has never been expressly abolished by law.

The ancient stocks at Ottery St Mary are now carefully preserved under a canopy within the churchyard (Plate 15), and they are a reminder of the rough justice of former days.

The pound

The common pound was an enclosure set apart for detaining stray animals, particularly cattle, which in the times of 'open-fields' often trespassed on to neighbouring land.

They could be taken to the pound, and kept there until the owner paid for any damage they had caused. He was also fined, and these payments augmented the income of the lord of the manor, for the pound belonged to him. Animals and goods could be seized and impounded for non-payment of rent, and kept in the pound until redeemed.

The pound at Ottery St Mary was on the east side of Butts Hill (now called North Street).

The factory

Towards the end of the 18th century it was decided to build a factory near the town mill in Mill Street to manufacture serges, known as 'long ells', for the East India Company. The foundation stone was laid by Sir George Yonge, bart. and John Duntze in 1788. Sir George Yonge was Secretary of State for War, and lived at Escot House.

By the following year the factory was completed at a cost of £40,000. It was about this time that the mill stream was enlarged, and the 'Tumbling Weir' constructed to return the water to the river Otter. This basin type of weir is believed to be unique. The large waterwheel, 18ft. in diameter, was thought to be the largest in England at that time.

But the great days of the Devonshire cloth industry were almost over, and the French Revolution, followed by the Napoleonic Wars, dealt a heavy blow to the trade. There had been some promise of revival by selling the serges to the East India Company which, in turn, sold them to China. Although the Rev. Daniel Lysons, writing in 1822, stated that Ottery St Mary had 'a large manufactory for spinning wool', the trade was on the decline.[1] The terms were uneconomic, and with the building of large mills and factories in the North, the introduction of steam power, and greatly improved machinery, the woollen industry gradually moved to Yorkshire.

By 1823 it was not surprising to find that the manufacture of serges at Ottery St Mary was superseded by the development of a silk industry, which was soon flourishing. The main articles made were handkerchiefs and ribands.

The threat of invasion, 1803–05

By the turn of the century England was under the threat of imminent invasion by Napoleon's army, and the whole countryside was alerted. The danger had become very real, and a system of semaphore signals from hill tops was arranged to give warning of any landing.

On the north side of the town was a shooting range, where volunteers were undergoing military training. The road leading into the town from Honiton, now known as North Street, was called Butts Hill after the butts or mounds behind the targets and, of more recent date, there is Butts Road.

Lieutenant-General J. G. Simcoe of Wolford Lodge, north of Honiton, who had been the first Governor of Upper Canada, was placed in command of the volunteers and militia in this part of Devon. In 1803, temporary barracks were built in a field across the river Otter near St Saviour's Bridge, to the west of the town. This field became known as 'the Barrack Field', and the road leading up out of the valley towards Exeter is still called Barrack Hill. With these signs of military activity, Ottery St Mary for a time resembled a garrison town! When the invasion scare eventually passed with the Treaty of Paris, and the retirement of Napoleon to Elba in 1814, the barracks were dismantled.

Dorothea Mundy's gift

In 1807 Dorothea Mundy, by a codicil to her will, bequeathed to the governors of the church the sum of £50 secured by deed poll on the tolls of the Exeter turnpike roads, and she directed that the interest should be distributed on Christmas Day each year among eight elderly and deserving poor people of the parish, who attended the church regularly and were communicants there. A certificate stating their names and confirming their regular attendance at divine service has to be supplied by the vicar.

Great storms

In 1808 the 16th-century Cadhay Bridge was swept away by the rushing waters of the river Otter during a great storm, which also destroyed Fenny Bridge. It was in the autumn of 1824 that severe storms again struck the coasts of Devon and Cornwall, and the heavy rains caused the river to rise above its banks. The flood waters swept down the valley, and Gosford Bridge was washed away. Then, during the great storm on Tuesday, 23 November, the massive Chit Rock at Sidmouth was swept away by the raging seas, together with a row of old cottages on the beach. It was on this memorable occasion that, according to Sydney Smith, the dauntless Mrs. Partington stood in her cottage doorway attempting in vain to defy the ocean with a mop![2]

Restoration of the altar screen 1829–33

Churches throughout Devon had been allowed to fall into a sad state of dilapidation and neglect. When the redoubtable Henry Phillpotts became Bishop of Exeter in 1831, the whole diocese was in a deplorable state, and nearly half the parishes were without a resident incumbent.

In 1829 attention was at last turned to restoring the altar screen of Ottery church, which had been made 'a playne walle with morter and plaster' by order of Queen Elizabeth I's Commissioners nearly three hundred years before. The royal architect, Edward Blore (1787–1879), was engaged to ascertain whether it was possible to restore the front of the screen to its former medieval splendour.[3] There had originally been five large panels above the altar, each portraying in rich colours clouds and sky studded with stars, but on removing the plaster from the surface it was found impossible to restore them. So Blore decided to make three new panels with ornamental hoods, and 23 niches, but these remained empty and bare for the next 100 years.

During the closing years of the Georgian period the Wesleyan movement was spreading widely, and the religious life of the country was being transformed. A Methodist church was built in Mill Street, Ottery St Mary in 1829.

Chapter Nine

'MY NATIVE HOME'

AS WE HAVE SEEN in Chapter Six, the Rev. John Coleridge came to Ottery St Mary in August 1760 on his appointment as master of the King's School, and by the end of that year he had also become vicar of the parish.

By his first marriage he had three daughters, but they do not figure in his life at Ottery St Mary. His wife died, and in 1753, he married Ann Bowden at the church of St Mary Arches, Exeter. They had 10 children, the youngest being Samuel Taylor Coleridge, who was born on Wednesday, 21 October 1772 at the School House[1] about 11 o'clock in the morning. He was baptized at Ottery church on 30 December that year, and was named after his godfather, Samuel Taylor, who lived nearby and was a close friend of the family.

At the age of three, 'Sam', as he was called, was sent to a reading school kept by Dame Key, 'because I was too little to be trusted among my Father's schoolboys'. But his early childhood, according to his later recollections, appears to have been unhappy, as he was often tormented and bullied by the other boys, and so withdrew into a lonely dream-world of his own. He was a sensitive, introspective child, who absorbed himself in his books and read incessantly. As he was later to explain in autobiographical letters to his friend Thomas Poole:

> . . . I used to lie by the wall and mope, and my spirits used to come upon me suddenly; and in a flood of them I was accustomed to race up and down the Church-yard, and act over all I had been reading, on the docks, the nettles and the rank grass . . .

His favourite aunt, Susannah, kept a general stores at Crediton, which he amusingly referred to as 'an everything shop'.[2] He enjoyed his visits to her, for he was able to read through 'all the gilt-cover little books that could be had at that time'.

On an evening in late October 1779 in consequence of a quarrel with his brother Frank (Francis), Sam ran away from fear of being whipped, and passed the whole night, a night of rain and storm, on the bleak side of a hill by the river Otter.[3] It is unlikely that he would have run through the streets of the town on that autumn evening for, being the vicar's son, he would have been easily recognised. He may have darted out through the adjoining grounds of the Chanter's House (then called Heath's Court) and, on reaching the river, decided to hide below the hillside beyond the head weir. Although the actual spot where he spent that fateful night must be a matter of conjecture, this would fit in with his own description of the incident written many years afterwards.

Fig. 8. The Rev. John Coleridge with his horse by the choristers' hospice and college gate. (From a contemporary water-colour, c.1775.)

An anxious search was made throughout the night, and at daybreak Sam was found 'about six yards from the naked bank of the river', where he lay wet, cold, and unable to move. He was carried home to his overjoyed parents, and was later to recall how a young woman had rushed into the house, and cried out: 'I hope you'll whip him, Mrs. Coleridge!'. Whenever he saw that woman afterwards he could not overcome his antipathy towards her.

Before Sam was nine years old his father died suddenly after a visit to Plymouth, where he had taken Frank to join his ship as a midshipman under Admiral Thomas Graves, a friend of the family, who lived at Cadhay (*see* Chapter Eleven). The Rev. John Coleridge was buried on the north side of the chancel, before the altar screen of his church.

Mrs. Coleridge and her family moved out of the School House to make way for her husband's successor, and took up residence in the nearby Warden's House. As a poor widow, she found it difficult to maintain and educate her large family without assistance, and so she decided to apply to the Governors of Christ's Hospital in London to admit her youngest son 'there to be Educated, and brought up among other poor children'. And so, in April 1782, a place having been procured, Sam left his home for London.

This sad departure was to cut him off from those years of early childhood, and henceforth he found himself

> Still most a stranger, most with naked heart,
> At my own home and birthplace.

The loss of his father, who had been the only member of the family capable of understanding him, left Sam bereft of the companionship, which at such an impressionable age, was so essential to him. The 'poor friendless boy', as Charles Lamb, his junior at Christ's Hospital, described him, found himself far from his home and among some six hundred boys.

During his nine long years at Christ's Hospital his thoughts often turned to his birthplace, and those childhood days in the Devon countryside. He had been so young when he left Ottery St Mary that he was later to reflect 'most of those endearing circumstances that are wont to render the scenes of childhood in the recollection' were to be associated with Christ's Hospital rather than his home.

He appears to have made a brief visit to Ottery St Mary in the summer of 1789, for in a poem *Life,* written in September of that year, he described the countryside as he approached his birthplace.

> As late I journey'd o'er the extensive plain
> Where native Otter sports his scanty stream,
> Musing in torpid woe a Sister's pain,
> The glorious prospect woke me from the dream.
>
> At every step it widen'd to my sight—
> Wood, Meadow, verdant Hill, and dreary Steep,
> Following in quick succession of delight,—
> Till all—at once—did my eye ravish'd sweep!

As a result of his prodigious reading since early childhood, Coleridge had acquired a remarkable command of words, and throughout his life was to be an impassioned talker, who could hold his listeners enthralled. When writing of him many years later, his lifelong friend, Charles Lamb, described how he had 'seen the casual passer through the cloisters stand still with admiration . . . while the walls of the old Grey Friars re-echoed to the accents of the inspired charity boy!'.

When the time came to leave Christ's Hospital it was with feelings of affection, and in a farewell sonnet to his school it was inevitable that his thoughts should turn to that earlier parting.

> Farewell parental scenes! a sad farewell!
> To you my grateful heart still fondly clings . . .
> Lingering I quit you, with as great a pang
> As when erewhile, my weeping childhood, torn
> By early sorrow from my native seat,
> Mingled its tears with hers—my widow'd Parent lorn.

He decided to return to his home before going on to Cambridge to take up a small University Exhibition. But the visit was not a happy one for he was bitterly disillusioned by 'the manners of the Inhabitants', most of whom had forgotten him during his 'long exile'. Moreover, to add to his depression, his brother Luke, who had set up in practice as a doctor in Thorverton, Devon, had recently died at the early age of 24, leaving a young widow and small child surviving him. In March 1791 his only sister, Ann, had also died, aged 21, and was buried in the churchyard at Ottery St Mary.

While at Cambridge he got hopelessly into debt, and on visiting his birthplace early in August 1793, he feared that he would incur his brothers' displeasure. However, they helped him to resolve his difficulties, and even his eldest brother, James, was more amenable than he had dared to hope. But life was not all gloom, for he managed to visit some of the old haunts of his childhood.

About a mile south of the town is a sandstone cavern by the river Otter, which is known as Pixies' Parlour. Writing of this in the preface to *Songs of the Pixies*, Coleridge described how 'the roots of the old trees form its ceiling', and on returning there he was delighted to discover his initials, S.T.C., and those of his brothers, which had been 'cut by the hand of childhood'. He went on to relate that in summer 1793 he had taken a party of young ladies to Pixies' Parlour, and one of them 'of stature elegantly small, and of complexion colourless yet clear, was proclaimed the Faery Queen'. In his early poems Coleridge made frequent reference to his 'native home', and recalled fond memories of the river Otter, upon whose banks he had so often played as a child. Some of the most beautiful lines about the river Otter appear in his *Songs of the Pixies*:

> Then with quaint music hymn the parting gleam
> By lonely Otter's sleep-persuading stream;
> Or where his wave, with loud unquiet song
> Dashed o'er the rocky channel froths along;
> Or where, his silver waters smoothed to rest,
> The tall tree's shadow sleeps upon his breast.

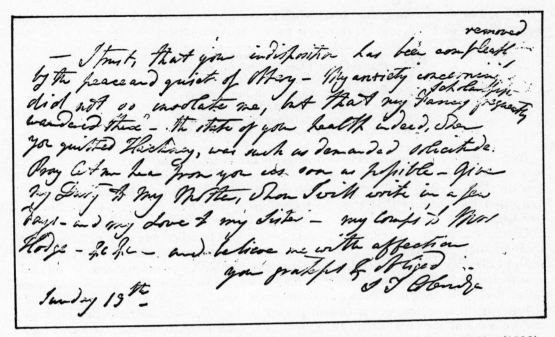

Fig. 9.   Facsimile of a letter from S.T. Coleridge to his brother, the Rev. George Coleridge (1793).

Nostalgic memories were recalled by Coleridge in *Sonnet to the River Otter*, written about that same year, in which he tells of those carefree days when he played 'ducks-and-drakes', skimming 'the smooth thin stone' upon the surface of its waters, and how, when he closed his eyes in the bright sunshine, he pictured the colourful tints of the river and its sandy bed, the plank bridge, and 'the willows grey', which grew upon its banks. And then, dismissing these visions as vain thoughts, he added, with a wishful sigh, 'Ah! that once more I were a careless child!'.

Some of his finest verse is contained in *The Rime of the Ancient Mariner*, and it was the gentle trickle of a West-Country stream that inspired those enchanting lines:

> A music like of a hidden brook
> In the leafy month of June,
> That to the sleeping woods all night
> Singeth a quiet tune.

It was not until towards the end of July 1796 that he made his next visit to his birthplace. It seemed a favourable opportunity to do so, for he was now married and had at last found a settled home. His brother James, known as 'the Colonel', was in course of purchasing the Chanter's House (then called Heath's Court). Of his reception by the family, Coleridge wrote: 'I was received by my Mother with transport, and by my brother George with joy and tenderness, & by my other brothers with affectionate civility'.

He was in a contemplative mood when he composed *Frost at Midnight* during the early months of 1798, and his thoughts turned again to Ottery St Mary:

> . . . I dreamt
> Of my sweet birth-place, and the old church-tower
> Whose bells, the poor man's only music, rang
> From morn to evening, all the hot Fair-day,
> So sweetly, that they stirred and haunted me
> With a wild pleasure, falling on mine ear
> Most like articulate sounds of things to come!

In September 1799 Coleridge came with his wife Sara to visit the family, and was accompanied by Robert Southey and his wife Edith, who was Sara's sister. It was on this occasion that Southey saw the Sherman epitaphs in Ottery church, and expressed the opinion that they had been composed by the poet William Browne (*see* Chapter Eleven).

Coleridge's mother was now 73 years of age and had become very deaf. Southey recalled that they had '. . . all been a good deal amused by the old lady', who, on seeing Coleridge arguing with his brothers, but unable to hear what was being said, assumed that he must have been in the wrong, and exclaimed: 'Ah, if your poor father had been alive, he'd soon have convinced you'.

But with the passing years, Coleridge was to find that his brothers had changed, and he was much dismayed by their opinions. To his consternation, he heard them speak in favour of slavery. He realised that if his visit was to be a success, he must not express his opinions too openly. Of his brothers, he wrote: 'George and the Colonel good men as times go—very good men—but alas! we have neither tastes nor feelings in common'.

At the end of June 1800 he moved to the Lake District to be near the Wordsworths. His marriage was unhappy and, although he was about to come south on a visit to Ottery St Mary in 1807 with Sara and the children, his brothers refused to receive him on learning that he intended to separate from his wife. He wrote a confidential letter to his favourite brother George with a very open explanation that he had decided to part from Sara, and giving his reasons. But soon the whole family knew, and rejected him. His reply was a 'downright red hot letter' to George, and several years were to pass before the rift with his brothers was eventually healed. But never again was Coleridge to return to his 'native place'.

He is regarded as Ottery St Mary's most famous son, and in him Devon had produced a literary genius. Although he had left the West Country, it was to that part of England that he truly belonged.

The last 18 years of his life were spent as a guest 'honoured and cherished' at the home of the kindly Dr. James Gillman and his wife at No. 3 The Grove, Highgate Village. He died there on 25 July 1834, aged sixty-one.

Chapter Ten

VICTORIAN OTTERY

Wordsworth's visit

FRANCIS GEORGE COLERIDGE (1794-1854) was a younger son of Colonel James Coleridge, and practised as a solicitor in the town. Among his many appointments was that of clerk to the local magistrates, and it was said of him that he 'became the trusted legal adviser of the whole countryside'. He showed great devotion to his church, and was a churchwarden.

After living for a while at The Lodge on Church Hill, he moved to The Cottage in Hind Street, which belonged to his father, and later bought the Manor House, where he died in 1854. His quiet, unassuming manner endeared him to all who knew him, and by his death the whole district lost 'a valued and beloved friend'.

On coming into the church one afternoon towards the end of May 1841, he had noticed a tall elderly gentleman. Thinking that he was an interested visitor, he approached him and was surprised to find he was the celebrated poet William Wordsworth. He gave him a warm welcome, and invited him to tea with his family at the Manor House.

Wordsworth had travelled from the Lake District to make farewell visits to his old haunts in the Quantocks after an absence of over 40 years, and had decided to include the birthplace of his friend of former years, Samuel Taylor Coleridge. It is believed that this was the only occasion on which he came to Ottery St Mary.

The penny post

The introduction of the penny post by Rowland Hill in 1840 soon proved a great success despite early opposition. It is interesting to note that within four years of this service being established, more than 79,000 letters, and 12,200 newspapers passed through Ottery post office in a year. There were no letter boxes, so all letters had to be handed in at the post office in Mill Street, which was open from 8 a.m. until 8 p.m. daily, and between 8 a.m. and 10 a.m. on Sundays.

The Electric Telegraph Company was formed in 1846 and the growth of this valuable service was rapid. On 25 January 1871 the electric telegraph was opened at Ottery St Mary.

Waywardens

Roads were mostly rough and uneven, thick with dust during the summer, and muddy with deep ruts in winter. It was often necessary for two horses to pull a vehicle, where normally one would have been sufficient but for the deplorable state of the roads. In the town, poultry and even pigs strayed about among the farm carts and gigs. Sandhill Street was in the 18th century also known as Pigs Street, presumably because the inhabitants there were mainly pig keepers.

It was only the main roads which were paved or metalled, and these were not good. Where there was a 'High Street' in a town, this was the principal street, and, being raised to a higher level, it drained quicker than the less important roads.

Four persons known as 'waywardens' were appointed annually at the courts-baron of the manor of Ottery to superintend the upkeep of the roads of the parish. There was a waywarden responsible for the town area, and he was required to reside in the town. Three waywardens, who were usually farmers, were appointed for the country districts.

It is recorded in the court rolls that on 30 September 1736, the jury presented

> That the Waywardens had suffered the Cornhill, Flexton, Mill Street, and several other streets to be much out of order in the pavement. Ordered that they do putt the same in good repair before the first day of November next under the penalty of 6s. 8d. [33p].

And at a court-leet and court-baron of the manor held on 3 May 1739, it was presented

> That the Waywardens ought to put a Bridge over the Lake called Combe Lake near Taleford. Ordered that the Waywardens do put up a Bridge on or before the 20 of this Instant May under the penalty of 6s. 8d.

A sum of about £220 was spent each year upon the upkeep of the roads of the parish, towards which the town contributed £75. Within the town area there were about six miles of the most hilly and expensive roads, and it frequently happened that the town waywarden found himself with insufficient funds to enable him to carry out all the necessary repair work. The most commonly used material for road-mending was flint gravel, which was taken from the bed of the river and carted by local farmers at a reasonable charge.

Waywardens' accounts for the years 1830 to 1844 are carefully preserved among the records of the church corporation.

Railways

In the spring of 1844 the railway came to Devon. The Bristol and Exeter Railway was a continuation of the Great Western Railway from Bristol, and was opened on 1 May 1844 amidst great public rejoicing. The first train did the 194-mile journey from Paddington to Exeter in exactly five hours.

The old order of things was to change with the coming of the railways, and many market towns, which had formerly been prosperous, faced a loss of trade, and a drift of population to the larger towns served by main lines. The nearest stations to Ottery St Mary were Cullompton and Hele, and it was essential to have contact with them if the town was to survive as a thriving community. Accordingly, two carriers plied between Ottery St Mary and these stations each week. The carriers' carts were an important means of communication.

In addition, there were carriers in Ottery St Mary, who travelled to Exeter on Tuesdays and Fridays. Sarah Pike, who was a carrier in Mill Street, went to Honiton on Saturdays, and to Sidmouth on Mondays. The *Telegraph* stage coach left the *Old London Inn*, Exeter at 5 a.m. every day, except Sunday, taking 17 hours for the journey to London. The fare was 35s. 0d. (£1.75) if you travelled on the outside of the coach; otherwise if was £3 10s. 0d. (£3.50) for an inside seat.

It was not until 1 August 1860 that the extension of the London and South Western Railway from Yeovil was at last completed, so linking Waterloo Station with Exeter. The branch line to Sidmouth, which served Ottery St Mary, did not follow until 1874, but this was regrettably 'axed' as a result of the Beeching Report in 1967.

St Saviour's bridge

An old print (Plate 16) shows that St Saviour's bridge, which spans the river Otter, was originally an attractive hump-back bridge containing four small arches. It was swept away during a severe storm on the night of Friday, 7 December 1849, and was replaced by the iron structure we have today, which was built a little further downstream. The line of the road leading into the town from the direction of Exeter was altered, so as to make a wider sweep into Mill Street than had formerly been the case.

Thackeray's *Pendennis*

William Makepeace Thackeray (1811–63) during his Charterhouse days (1825–28) had spent part of his school holidays with his step-father, Major Carmichael Smyth, who lived at Larkbeare House. When writing *The History of Pendennis,* which followed his successful novel *Vanity Fair,* Thackeray recalled memories of those holidays of more than twenty years before, and his impressions of this corner of Devon.

Ottery St Mary is clearly identified with that 'little old town of Clavering St Mary', the birthplace of Arthur Pendennis. The river Otter is called the 'River Brawl'; Sidmouth appears as 'Baymouth', and Exeter as 'Chatteris'.

The Wapshot boys are described as making a good cheerful noise, scuffling with their feet as they marched into church and scampered up the organ loft stairs. Thackeray may have heard during those holidays at Larkbeare how the boys of the King's School used to jostle and clatter up the steps to take their places on the rood loft above the 'broad and solid' stone screen, then at the entrance to the chancel of Ottery church, where they sat during divine service. This rood screen had been about 10ft. in height and 6ft. in depth, with a stone staircase leading up to the rood loft or 'pulpitum'.

Thackeray did his own delightful illustrations for his novels, and in the first edition of *Pendennis,* which was published serially in monthly parts in bright yellow covers, there is a vignette of the north tower of Ottery church.

Restoration of the church

In 1841, the Exeter Diocesan Architectural Society, after making an inspection of the parish church, reported that it had a degraded and neglected appearance. For some years the condition of the interior had been a source of profound regret, and almost shame. The vital question of restoration was at last occupying the minds of certain parishioners, and in 1846 Sir John Taylor Coleridge (known as 'the Judge') launched an appeal. After long negotiations, the restoration and re-arrangement of the entire interior of the church began on 21 May 1849.

The work was entrusted to William Butterfield (1814–1900), a zealous Victorian restorer obsessed with a colour theory 'that such combinations were permissible as could be produced by uncoloured natural materials'. The church, having once been a collegiate foundation, was not conveniently built for use as a parish church. The chancel and also the transepts were on a higher level than the nave, so that when the church became used for parochial worship, some of the congregation were raised nearly three feet above the rest, which was a most inconvenient arrangement.

Butterfield determined not only to bring the floor of the transepts down to the same level as the nave but to extend this eastwards towards the altar screen. This was to prove a considerable undertaking, and the excavation and removal of the sandstone to reduce the level of the floor was a harder task than at first envisaged. The bases of the first columns on either side of the nave still clearly show the line of the original floor level.

The vaulting of the church (except the Dorset aisle), and the ceilings of the chapels of St Stephen and St Lawrence, were richly adorned with colour, and the bosses were gilded. The remaining Tudor bench ends were assembled together in the Dorset aisle, where we find them today.

The old octagonal font, at which Samuel Taylor Coleridge had been baptized, was described in 1841 as being 'in a great state of dilapidation but not so entirely defaced as to render it impossible to trace its design (see Fig. 10). When it was removed during the restoration work, there was found beneath it a block of Purbeck stone, which may well have formed the base of the original Norman font. Upon this was placed the ponderous square font specially designed by Butterfield. It was his object to use marble in church work to obtain an effective result of rich natural colour. Apart from the white pieces, all the marble used for this multi-coloured effect came from Devon and Cornwall. The final result was considered to be 'a sumptuous and beautiful work' much admired by the Victorians.

The entire work of restoration was carried out by local craftsmen under the superintendence of Butterfield, and was completed in less than 12 months. Moreover, it was remarkable, when the extent of the work is considered, to find that the church was open for three full services every Sunday, and daily prayer was suspended for only one week.

As dawn broke on Wednesday, 15 May 1850, the church bells pealed out to herald a day of celebration and thanksgiving on the accomplishment of the restoration. And the weather, too, favoured this great day, which was filled with a crowning sense of achievement.

On 11 September 1851, a decade
after the Exeter Diocesan Architectural Society had made that report
on the sorry state of the church, John
Duke Coleridge, eldest son of Sir
John Taylor Coleridge, addressed the
members of the society on the restoration work, and went on to
describe the church as 'almost unsurpassed among other Churches of its
size, for the majestic austerity of
its design . . . all is plain and severe,
but stately and dignified in no ordin-
ary measure'.

District churches

During the first half of the 19th
century the population of Ottery
St Mary had almost doubled, and by
1851 there were 4,500 inhabitants,
which exceeded the populations of
Honiton and Sidmouth respectively
by one thousand.

With this growth in population,
churches were needed for the neighbouring districts. By 1840, small

Fig. 10.   The old font at which Samuel Taylor
Coleridge was baptised on 30 December 1772.
It was replaced by William Butterfield's ponder-
ous marble font in 1850.

churches had been built at Escot and Tipton St John. The first stone of the
church of St Michael the Archangel at West Hill was laid on 6 October 1845
by Sir J. T. Coleridge, whose nephew, George B. Wollaston, was the architect.
The church was built of stone in the Early English style, and was consecrated
by the redoubtable Henry Phillpotts, Bishop of Exeter (1831–69) on Michaelmas
Day 1846. At first it was a chapel of ease in Fluxton tithing with about 220
parishioners, but a parish was later assigned to it, and it became a benefice with
its own vicar. In February 1983 West Hill was included within the Otter Vale
team ministry.

Sir J. T. Coleridge gave a piece of land at Alfington as a site for a church there,
built in accordance with designs prepared by William Butterfield. In addition, the
judge provided a residence and stipend for the minister, and built a school house
at his own expense. The little church was dedicated to St James and St Anne, and
was opened under the bishop's licence in 1849, but was not consecrated until
Michaelmas Day 1882, over 33 years later.

John Coleridge Patteson (1827–71) was a nephew of the church's benefactor,
being the eldest son of Frances Duke Coleridge, who had married Sir John Patteson
of Feniton Court. He was ordained in Exeter Cathedral in 1853, and became curate

at Alfington in Ottery parish, where he remained for the next two years, but left to devote himself to missionary work among the islands of the South Pacific.

In 1861 he was made first Bishop of Melanesia, and met a martyr's death, when he was killed by the natives on the small island of Nakapu on 20 September 1871. A memorial at the west end of Alfington church records his ministry and tragic death, and at Spence Cross, where the Ottery St Mary to Feniton road crosses the busy A30, a wayside cross of red brick and stone was erected to his memory. In the nave of Exeter Cathedral is the martyr's pulpit, which was designed in stone by Sir Gilbert Scott, and set up by public subscription in 1877 in memory of Bishop Patteson. His martyrdom forms the central panel, while to the left is St Alban, and on the right St Boniface.

Social conditions

Ottery St Mary, like other small towns, was still a compact, self-contained community with its church, chapels, schools, mills, fairs, and every kind of shop, craft and trade. In fact, the parish was the orbit of most people's lives. The inhabitants made their own entertainments, and had their amusements and interests. There was the town band, bell-ringing, national festivals, and fairs, as well as various sports.

The town had the reputation of being the centre of one of the best dairy districts in Devon. Among the trades and occupations to be found were 13 drapers, dressmakers, milliners and outfitters, including a straw bonnet maker, and three Honiton lace manufacturers, although this industry was on the decline. In addition to these were six tailors, and no less than 17 boot and shoemakers. As for food, there were seven grocers, 11 bakers, six butchers, a fishmonger, and a potato merchant. Other occupations included millers, builders, blacksmiths, wheelwrights, chimney sweepers, thatchers, organ builders, watch and clock makers, and straw hat makers.

The manufacture of silk was carried on at the factory upon a considerable scale, and provided employment for over 400 men and women. The large waterwheel turned by the millstream worked 47 spinning frames, containing 2,256 spindles.

Among well-known names were Thomas Shepperd, who carried on the family business of a grocer, wine and spirit merchant and draper in Silver Street; almost opposite was William Whicker's bakery business, which was carried on there for more than a hundred years by the Whicker family. There was John Coles, the saddler and harness maker in Cornhill, and William Henry Godfrey, the boot and shoemaker. William Digby and Henry Williams were both butchers, and Edward Gover carried out the dual duties of town crier and also sexton (officially known as 'the Bedman').

Some more unusual trades at that time included a cooper, or maker of casks; a whitesmith, who worked in tin; a brazier, who worked in brass; a tanner, who made leather from raw hides, and a currier, who dressed the tanned leather.

Wages

A couple of ducks could be bought for 4s. 0d. (20p), and eggs were 6d. (2½p) a dozen. Butter cost 1s. 0d. (5p) a pound. Beef was 6½d.(3p) a pound, and a choice leg of pork could be had at 5d.(2p) a pound.

Although the cost of living in the mid-19th century may seem low to us today, wages were lamentably small, and the poorer classes had a hard struggle to exist without some help from the parish. An agricultural labourer was paid from 7s. 0d. (35p) to 9s. 0d.(45p), if he worked a full week. This meant starting at 6 o'clock each morning, and working until 5.30 p.m., and until 4 p.m. on Saturdays. Those labourers who lived in the town paid 1s. 4d. (7p) or 1s. 6d. (7½p) a week for rent, but those living on the farms usually gave a day's work to the farmer in lieu of rent. During the winter months many were unemployed, but some were able to find work upon the roads at 10d (4p) to 1s. 0d. (5p) a day.

Young women at the silk factory worked hard to earn 5s. 0d (25p) a week, whilst piece workers could make as much as 8s. 0d. (40p), but had to be good hands. They worked 10 hours a day, and many of them lodged in overcrowded conditions in small houses in the town. They could not afford to be ill, otherwise their rent and shop bills fell into arrears, and they might be driven into the workhouse.

A possible topic of polite conversation

If we take the average age of all those who died during the three years 1846, 1847 and 1848, it is found to be 24 years. Of the 93 deaths during the year 1848, 21 of these were due to cholera, and contagious diseases, and a further 31 were children under five years of age. Infant mortality was still heavy, and the insanitary conditions and appalling overcrowding of the houses of the poorer inhabitants contributed considerably towards this.

In 1849, a preliminary inquiry was held to investigage the state of the drainage, water supply and sanitation of the town, and a report was made to the General Board of Health the following year. In general, there was no such thing as a system of drainage, and the town was seldom, if ever, free from cases of what was then referred to as 'low fever', or 'typhus fever'. There had been serious outbreaks of cholera in 1832 and again in 1848.

Where the sewage and house-refuse was carried off at all, this was by means of open ditches or gutters, which discharged into the main streams passing from east to west through the midst of the town. The main brook was the Teap stream, which came down from Little Well, and passed between Sandhill Street and Yonder Street, eventually discharging its filth and garbage into what was called 'Mud Pit' in Hind Street. This was emptied about once a year, and the black soil used on nearby land, where a system of sewage irrigation had been effected on a small scale.

The scavenger, who was appointed annually to cleanse the streets of the town, was unpaid, but could sell the refuse he collected. Consequently, it was his practice to deposit this in a vacant space in the public street opposite his house, where it accumulated until he sold it. William Reed had a boarding school in Broad Street, and complained that he was placed between two nuisances. The common open gully passed within six feet of the playground wall after receiving sewage from half the town, and the scavenger's manure heap was deposited within 23 feet of his front door!

There were five public pumps providing water for drinking purposes, and in many cases the inhabitants had to go a considerable distance to fetch it. These were in Mill Street, Broad Street, Sandhill Street, Yonder Street, and in Paternoster Row. A charge of 1d. (½p) per quarter was made towards the cost of keeping the pumps in repair, but when default in payment was made, the handles were locked down. It was stated at the inquiry that 'hardly a quarter passes without the supply being thus more or less cut off', and this was sometimes for long periods.

Following the report of the inquiry into these deplorable conditions, an Order in Council was made on 13 July 1850 for the setting up of a Local Board of Health. This was to consist of nine members, six of whom were elected from the town area, and the other three from the outlying districts of the parish.

A water supply was brought to the town in 1852, but the awakening of public interest in the vital matter of sanitation came slowly. Little was done about improving drainage and water systems until a further outbreak of cholera in 1865–66 brought matters to a head. Local authorities were compelled to appoint sanitary inspectors, and to undertake the provision of sewers and refuse disposal.

Although attempts were made to introduce public street lighting, these were continually frustrated. Many streets were narrow and winding, but there were no public lights whatever until eventually the town was lighted by gas in 1865.

Another commission prepared a statement of the basic conditions 'necessary for civilized social life' and, following this, the Local Government Board (whose functions are now performed by the Department of Health and Social Security) was established to enforce the law relating to public health.

The subject of drains had at last become a possible topic of polite conversation, and one upon which the public was becoming knowledgeable.

Markets

After the destruction by fire of the old market hall in 1767 (*see* p. 81) a new structure was erected at the top of what was then known as Church Hill, near the site now occupied by the red-brick town hall. On market day farmers and their wives from the surrounding country districts brought in their butter packed in tubs, eggs, bacon and other produce. This was displayed for sale on trestles inside this market house, which was open on all sides.

The butchers congregated together in their particular corner of the Flexton, known as 'the Shambles' (or 'fleshambles'), so called from the stalls set up there for the sale of meat. This weekly market was held on Tuesdays, but was later changed to Thursdays.

A cattle market was held every month, and the cattle and sheep were sold on Church Hill, in The Flexton, and in Broad Street. Sheep were also placed in pens along the length of The College. The hurdles required on market days were stored in the old building near the entrance to The College, which was also used as a lock-up for drunks until the police could attend to them!

There were three annual fairs for the sale of cattle, and quantities of cheese were sold at the August fair. There was also a regular corn market. All these fairs and markets were an important feature in the life of the town, with the market house as the busy centre.

By the middle of the 19th century the market house had become derelict. The tolls, fees and other advantages arising from the fairs and markets were paid to Sir John Kennaway of Escot, as lord of the manor, and he agreed to grant a 99-year lease of what was described as 'a piece of land then used as the Market Place and Shambles in the Town of Ottery St Mary' to the then newly-formed Ottery Town Hall and Market Trust. The present town hall was built on this site by the trustees, and was opened on 11 April 1860, with the object of providing a suitable place for 'Petty Sessions, and other public purposes, a retiring room, a library, a reading room and a more convenient Market'. The benefit of all fees and tolls was assigned to the Market Trust.

By the year 1878 the big cattle fairs had been reduced to two a year—on the last Thursdays in March and September, and they were eventually to lose their old character. Markets continued to be held on Church Hill and The Flexton, including the sale of cattle and sheep, until the end of the century.

On 6 October 1863 the tremors of an earthquake were felt in the early hours of the morning, and five years later there was another earthquake shock, but this was slight.

Some old inns

The inn forms an essential part of the life of every town and village, and historically and architecturally may contribute particular interest and atmosphere. The *London Hotel* was formerly known as the *London Tavern*. It was built early in the 18th century, and possibly replaced an earlier inn on the same site. In White's *History, Gazetteer and Directory of Devonshire* of 1878, it is described as 'a commercial and family hotel and posting House'. The magistrates' courts were held here on the third Thursday of every alternate month.

A central archway led through to the cobbled inn yard at the rear, but this was replaced by an improved entrance to the hotel in 1936, and an additional window put in to the right of it. The property was seriously damaged by fire in the early hours of 28 September 1982.

Reference is made to 'the Kings Arms in this Town' in a deed dated 1762. This inn is believed to have been built in 1756, and takes its name from the royal arms of George II. This was also a posting house where a change of horses could be obtained by travellers for the next stage of their journey.

The *Lamb and Flag Inn* in Batts Lane was a tavern of some importance, and possibly occupies the site of a religious hospice (*hospitium*) which may have stood here in medieval times, providing refreshment and lodging for pilgrims and wayfarers. The name is of religious significance, for it is derived from the *Agnus Dei*

—the holy lamb holding the banner with uplifted foot—the emblem of the risen Christ.

Among the other inns in the town in 1850 was the *Red Lion Inn* at the foot of Tiphill, which was destroyed by the great fire in 1866. The *Volunteer* in Broad Street bears a name derived from the patriotic fervour during the wars early in the 19th century. Then there was the *Half Moon Inn* on Butts' Hill (North Street), the *Masons' Arms* in Sandhill Street, and the *Five Bells* (now demolished), which stood in Mill Street.

A little more than a mile to the north-west of the town is the *Fairmile Inn,* which stands on the parish boundary. In his *History of Devonshire* (published 1793–1806), the Rev. Richard Polwhele wrote:

> A beam running through the kitchen has a mark in the middle of it—to show that one side of the kitchen lies in Ottery, and the other in Talaton.

The cricket club, 1858

There was an increasing interest in all forms of sport, and clubs were being formed throughout the country, particularly for cricket. In June 1858 the Ottery St Mary Cricket Club was founded, and in the following month its secretary was writing to the Exeter club saying that Ottery was 'desirous of Playing a Match, if you are disposed to accept a challenge from us'.

Batting gloves cost 5s. 0d. (25p) per pair, pads were 10s. 0d. (50p), and 'best match balls' cost 6s. 0d. (30p) each. If the ball was lost, it was agreed by the club that the finder should be paid 1s. 0d. (5p). A charge of 6d. (2½p) was made for every male spectator attending a match, but ladies were admitted free.

The first meetings of the cricket club were held at the *Red Lion Inn* in a large room called the club room.

The great fire of 1866

Most towns have at some stage in their history suffered disastrous fires, and Ottery St Mary is no exception. Of the four extensive fires within the last four centuries, the first is recorded on a fly leaf in the earliest parish register, and reads: 'On the Xth day of Julye An. Dni. 1604 was the lower end of the Towne of Otterye St. Marye consumed with fire'.

Close-built cottages with thatched roofs and many wooden buildings in the town made fire an ever-present risk. We find the Exeter city magistrates making an order for the relief of those who had suffered loss as a result of the 'painful pre-eminence in conflagrations', and the inhabitants of Heavitree, Exeter, 'Delivered unto Wm. Leigh, the constable of the parish, in August 1604, towards the relieving of such as had taken great loss by misfortune of fire at Otterye, xvi.s. [80p]'. In the churchwardens' accounts for Tavistock for 1605/06, there is an entry which reads: 'Itm. the ixth of April paid Robert Collyn for the Relief of the Towne of Otterye by an imposicion Layd downe by the Justices at the Chapter House iij li.xs.' (£3.50.)

A serious fire occurred in autumn 1716, but little is known about this, although the loss sustained amounted to £4,466. Collections were made by a number of towns, including some in the North, to relieve the distress.

On 16 March 1767, some 50 houses in the midst of the town were destroyed by the 'Great Fire', including the original market house, which was situated in The College on the east side of the King's School. The eastern gable of the school room prevented the flames reaching the Vicars' House.

The most disastrous fire occurred on Friday, 25 May 1866. It started shortly after midday in a cottage behind the National School in Jesu Street, and within four hours 111 houses had been destroyed, and 500 people rendered homeless. A great part of the town extending westwards from the school to the silk factory in Mill Street was reduced to a heap of smouldering ruins; partly collapsed walls stood blackened and charred, whilst chimney stacks pointed like gaunt fingers to the sky (*see* Fig. 11).

There had been a long period of dry weather. A fresh east wind rapidly fanned the flames along the thatched roofs of cob cottages in Jesu Street towards the *Red Lion Inn,* which stood at the corner of Tiphill. This inn, with its extensive stabling, was reached within an hour, by which time some 40 cottages were blazing fiercely on both sides of the road. The flames raged with relentless fury, destroying all but one of the houses on Tiphill, and leaving a scene of utter desolation. Furniture and personal possessions were flung from the windows by the desperate

Fig. 11.   Jesu Street, Ottery St Mary (looking west) after the Great Fire on 25 May 1866. (From a woodcut in *The Illustrated London News* **on 9 June 1866.)**

owners in a frantic effort to save them. People fled in terror from their burning homes dragging with them such articles as they could, and stacking these in the shelter of the church. The house of lawyer Davy in Broad Street (where the Marist Convent School now stands) was completely burnt out and, as he was away at the time, all his furniture went up in flames, too. The heat became so intense that trees and shrubs in the garden, as far as 50 yards away, were scorched.

The fire appears to have passed behind other·properties in Broad Street to continue with renewed fury in Mill Street, which suffered severely. The heat from the blazing houses made the street impassable at times. A large tannery on what is still known as Tanners Hill was completely destroyed but, by demolishing part of some buildings, the town mill was saved.

An old Ottery resident recalled how her grandfather was returning from Branscombe when, coming down East Hill, he saw a black cloud of smoke over the town. She added: 'He made what haste he could, for he was the Captain of the Fire Brigade'. But on reaching the town, he found that the small fire engine was out of action as the nozzle of the hose was blocked with mud, so an urgent request was made by telegraph to Exeter. At first this merely brought forth the reply that the Ottery engine was as good as theirs, so why should they come! However, after further persuasion, the Exeter fire brigade eventually set off with the horse-drawn fire engine, taking just over an hour to cover the 12-mile journey to Ottery St Mary. First, came the 'West of England' engine, to be followed by the 'Royal' and the 'Norwich' engines. The town had three fire engines, but these had, of necessity, to be small in order to reach the cottages, many of which were built in courtyards away from the streets, and had to be approached by narrow passageways. The old manual fire engine was not much larger than a perambulator, and was kept in a sandstone cavern in the west cliff near Tiphill Head.[1] The town's engines experienced great difficulty at first owing to lack of water, but after the Exeter fire engines arrived, they were able to pump some water from the river Otter.

When the flames had almost reached the silk factory, it was decided to pull down some intervening sheds to prevent the fire spreading further. So, after ceaseless effort in scenes of devastation, the conflagration was at last brought under control by 7.30 p.m. that evening. After many weeks of drought, it rained heavily on the day after the fire!

It was remarkable that, apart from some minor burns, there were no serious casualties among the inhabitants. An old lady, aged 92, had refused to abandon her cottage in which she had lived all her life until she was compelled to do so when flames came through the roof. In another case, a person had withdrawn £20 from his bank a fortnight previously and, although all appeared to have been lost, he recovered £3 10s. 0d. (£3.50) in gold, when sifting through rubbish a few days later.

The occupant of number 7 Mill Street, one of the few houses to escape, was Mrs. Godfrey, and she recorded the date of the fire by scratching this with a diamond ring upon a window pane at the rear of her house. This fragile memorial has been preserved, and recalls that day of terror and destruction.

Immediate steps were taken to find accommodation for. the homeless in other houses and buildings in the town. A public meeting was held, and financial and other assistance was given without delay to all those who had suffered loss.

Three months later there occurred an ironic sequel, for although the fire had been a catastrophe, there had been no loss of life or serious injury. On the evening of Sunday, 2 September, a woman preacher from Exeter was addressing a small gathering of people in the open air near the foot of Tiphill (on the site of the former Infants' School), and was attributing the recent fire to the wrath of God upon the people of Ottery St Mary for their sins! As she cried out, 'The rocks and the mountains shall fall upon us', the vibration of a heavy mail cart coming down Tiphill caused an isolated chimney stack among the ruined cottages on the site to collapse suddenly. It crashed upon the assembled crowd, killing eight people and injuring many others. Most of the victims had been standing listening to the preacher with the chimney stack immediately behind them. During the chaos which resulted, the 'prophetess' vanished, and was not heard of or seen again!

Foundation of the hospital

There is in the entrance hall of Ottery hospital a memorial tablet which records that Isabella Elizabeth Elliot, who died in 1902 in her 80th year, 'made it her home, watched over it with personal devotion and constant loving care and maintained it at her own cost for 22 years'. Mrs. Elliot had been left a widow at the comparatively early age of 48, and then, to add to her distress, she had lost her only child. She sought some way in which she might assuage the bitterness of her grief, and attempt to rebuild her shattered life, so she decided to create a small hospital where she could care for others.

On the recommendation of a friend, the Rev. Charles Kennaway, she came to Ottery St Mary, a place hitherto unknown to her. She approached a local doctor, Dr. Charles Whitby, and was soon to win his enthusiastic support for her plan. He took her to see Paxford House, a property in Lamb's Court, off Cornhill, which he thought might be made suitable for her purpose. She decided to purchase this property, and adapted it for use as a hospital. A sum of £50 was spent on providing surgical instruments, and four beds were given, but Mrs. Elliot declined any financial help.

On 1 December 1870 the hospital, such as it was, began its work with a staff consisting of a trained nurse and Mrs. Elliot's own cook and servants. There were three patients, but before long further improvements were made and seven beds were in use. These were early beginnings, and it was Mrs. Elliot's cherished ambition to establish a good working hospital of benefit to the town and district.

By October 1880 she was able to build a larger hospital on adjoining land, and this was completed in July 1882, when the patients were moved from Paxford House into more spacious wards.

This hospital continued under Mrs. Elliot's personal supervision until 1893 when, her financial resources exhausted, she decided to hand it over fully equipped, together with a large garden, to trustees to administer for the advantage of the town and surrounding district. Her noble work and generosity had ensured the

the continuance of a hospital, which has now served the community for well over a century.

The south transept 'beautified'

In December 1873, John Duke Coleridge (1820–94) was appointed Lord Chief Justice of the Court of Common Pleas (as it was then known), and was created first Baron Coleridge of Ottery St Mary. His father had retired in 1858 after being a Puisne Judge of the Queen's Bench for 23 years, and he spent the rest of his life at his home, Heath's Court (now the Chanter's House), where he died on 11 February 1876.

A Norman-style cross of Haytor granite was erected to his memory in the south-east corner of the churchyard by his many 'friends and neighbours'. Under the eastern window of the south transept of the church is an inscription, which reads:

> This Tower is beautified in pious memory of the Right Honourable Sir John Taylor Coleridge and Mary his wife, as a thank-offering to God from their reverent and grateful Son.

The services of William Butterfield, who was a friend of the Coleridge family, were once more engaged, and the walls of the south transept were covered with panels of tiled mosaics. The wooden gallery, upon which Bishop Grandisson's ancient clock stands, was repaired, and the interesting clock-face was carefully preserved. The windows in this transept were filled with stained-glass by members of the Coleridge family. Whilst this work of restoration was being carried out, the first Lady Coleridge (Jane Fortescue Seymour) died after a brief illness early in 1878, and in a recess on the east side of the transept is a beautiful recumbent figure of her in white marble, executed by Frederick Thrupp, R.A. At her feet is an otter, the Coleridge heraldic device.

The restoration of this transept was completed by 15 September 1878, and the following year the church was heated by hot air! In 1875 a new clock by Gillet and Bland was installed in the south tower, and replaced the former clock, which had a diamond-shaped dial. Then in 1887 two new treble bells were added to the peal.

Decline of the King's School

Through the years the fortunes of the King's School had fluctuated considerably, with successful periods in the mid–18th century and early in the next century, but by the time Queen Victoria came to the throne grammar schools generally were on the decline.[2] Times were changing, and the choice of schools had become wider as, with the coming of the railways, they were made more readily accessible.

Under the Rev. George Smith, who was appointed Master of the King's School in 1863, the number of pupils rapidly dwindled. He appears to have been more interested in farming than teaching.

A parliamentary inquiry was held in 1868 to look into the condition and useful-ness of the schools in Devon. Among the old grammar schools was the King's

School, and of this the Schools Inquiry Commission reported: 'The school is useless and cannot be said to be doing any work whatever'. There were only four boys in a dilapidated room with a few sticks of broken furniture and, in what should have been the boarders' dining room, two carriages were kept.

After some considerable persuasion, the Rev. George Smith eventually agreed to retire, although he showed the greatest reluctance to do so. And so, in 1881, this historic school closed down after almost 340 years. Early the following year, we find the governors reporting 'that the buildings are at this moment in a state requiring immediate attention to preserve them against weather'. In 1884, they were sold for £640, and shortly afterwards demolished, and included with them was the School House, where Coleridge had been born.

A scheme dated 19 July 1883 made under the Endowed Schools Act 1869 dealt with the administration of the endowments of the old school, and proposed that a site should be found so as to re-open the school at a future date. Meanwhile, the church governors were required to pay one-seventh of the yearly income of the church corporation for the benefit of the King's School. This annual payment has continued to the present day, so preserving a link with the original foundation.

There had been no national system of public education until 1870, when locally elected school boards were set up under the Elementary Education Act of that year. Ottery School Board was formed in November 1873, but new schools for girls and boys had been opened in the town in 1867 and 1868 respectively, and were now with compulsory attendance up to the age of thirteen. A Board School was opened at West Hill on 1 July 1876, to be followed by a Board Infant School in Ottery St Mary early the next year.

The King's School re-opens

Although the scheme of 1883 had envisaged rebuilding the King's School on a suitable site on the outskirts of the town, the governors decided early in 1894 to purchase The Priory. This Georgian house, which included 'a brewhouse, dairyhouse, stable and other outbuildings', was conveyed to them for £1,100. The Royal Assent was obtained in order to re-open the school there, and it started in January 1896. It was not long before the number of pupils had increased to such an extent that larger premises were needed. On 23 January 1912 the school moved into more extensive accommodation at Thorne on the western fringe of the town, which had been built for this purpose. And with this move, the King's School became the first co-educational grammar school in Devon.

Queen Victoria's Diamond Jubilee

There was public rejoicing for the Queen's Diamond Jubilee in 1897, and to commemorate the occasion a red-brick memorial was erected in a commanding position below the south wall of the churchyard at the head of Church Hill. It is believed to be a replica of one of the gateposts at the entrance to Kensington Gardens in London, and was often referred to as 'the other post'. This memorial stands on the site formerly occupied by the town stocks.

Chapter Eleven

THE BIG HOUSES

THE STORY of Ottery St Mary would not be complete unless something was said about 'the big houses', for their occupants have through the centuries made their particular contribution to the life and activities of the town and district. They are part of our history.

Ash

The ancient mansion of Ash was situate to the north of the parish near the Roman road leading from Honiton to Exeter, but today all that remains to preserve the name is Ash Farm and a few cottages.

In Henry III's reign (1216–72) the property belonged to Robert de Lupe. It passed by purchase to Lord William Bonville of Shute, and was eventually seized by the crown by way of fine. Ash was ultimately bought by Humphrey Walround, who resided there in early Stuart times, and died in December 1637. An ornate Jacobean monument to his memory was placed on the south wall of St Lawrence's chapel in the church. His second wife was Elizabeth Duke of Otterton, near East Budleigh, and the arms above this monument show those of Walround impaling those of Duke.

Ash later passed to the Pitt family of Coombe at Gittisham, and eventually went to the Markers, who succeeded them.

Cadhay

Of the 'big houses' situated among the pleasant farmland surrounding Ottery St Mary the fine Tudor mansion of Cadhay is the most notable. It stands about a mile to the north-west of the town, and its situation was quaintly described by Tristram Risdon, a Devon historian, writing in 1620, who said: '. . . it lieth also west over the River Tale, which here unloadeth itself into the River Otter'.

The name 'Cadhay' dates back to Saxon times, when the land was occupied by a Thane called Cada. It was Cada's 'enclosure', or land enclosed by a hedge (O.E. [ge]haeg or hege).

Early muniments of title mention Thomas de Cadehaye as being styled 'Dominus de Cadehaye' in 1320. Then in 1322 John de Cadehaye granted the estate to his brother, Richard, and his issue 'with all common pasture for his animals in all the moors and hills of Cadhay, and also turbary and furze . . .'.[1]

In 1432, the deeds refer to a Beatrix de Cadehaye and her son John as holding Cadhay. Henry de Cadehay is mentioned as having died in 1455, and the estate was eventually conveyed by a John de Cadehaye to trustees in 1483.

Joan de Cadhay married Hugh Grenville (or Grenefeld) and on the death of their son, Robert, Cadhay passed to his widow, Elyn. Her only daughter and heiress was Joan who, in 1527, married John Haydon of Ebford, near Topsham, in Woodbury parish. Cadhay was included in the marriage settlement and so was to pass to the Haydon family, who held it for the next 200 years.

John Haydon was a successful lawyer, and a bencher of Lincoln's Inn. We are told by Tristram Risdon in his *Survey of the County of Devon* that John Haydon '. . . builded at Cadhay a fair new house and enlarged his demesne'.[2] He was made a steward of the college property, and on the dissolution in 1545 he was appointed under the royal charter of Henry VIII to be one of the first governors of the parish church.[3]

When building his house at Cadhay, he appears to have made free use of the stone and other materials taken from the demolished chapter house and cloisters. He is known to have used some of the medieval stonework of other religious buildings in Exeter and the surrounding area, which likewise had been dissolved following the Reformation. He was, however, responsible for certain alterations to the south porch of Ottery church, where entry had formerly been from the cloisters (*see* Chapter Five).

The original Cadhay bridge was built to provide a crossing over the river Otter linking the newly-built mansion with the town. This bridge is believed to have borne an inscription which read 'John and Joan built me, pray good people repair me'.

It is almost certain that John Haydon's 'fair new house' was built upon the site of the original medieval hall house, which had been occupied by the de Cadehaye family.

By his will dated 12 February 1587 he expressed the wish to be 'buried in the Church of St Mary of Ottery on the north side of the Choir there', and he bequeathed the sum of 'forty shillings' (£2.00) for the maintenance of the church, and for his 'sepulchre there'. He died on 9 March 1587, without issue, and his wife, Joan, died in 1592.

The Easter sepulchre, to the immediate north of the altar, was built up into the Elizabethan tomb of John Haydon and his wife, and the quatrefoils on the side of the tomb were preserved from the original sepulchre. The manner in which the Easter sepulchre was worked up into the Haydon tomb may be clearly seen from the north choir aisle.

Cadhay passed to a great-nephew, Robert Haydon, the son of Thomas Haydon, and he was responsible for making a number of decorative additions to the property. He had also inherited several other family estates, and he married Joan, the eldest daughter of Sir Amyas Poulett of Hinton St George in Somerset, who had been ambassador to the French king, was made a privy councillor to Elizabeth I, and was the custodian of the unhappy Mary, Queen of Scots, during the three years leading to her execution in 1587.

Fig. 12

Arms of Paulet (or Poulett)

Sable, three swords pilewise
proper, pommels and hilts or.

(The swords of St Paul refer
to the name.)

Robert Haydon added the fine Tudor fireplace in the dining hall, which bears on its frieze of tracery the Poulett arms (*Sable, three swords pilewise proper, pommels and hilts or.*). The chimney piece is of Beer stone.

A long gallery was built on the south side of the house connecting the first floors of the east and west wings. This was a special feature of the late 16th and early 17th centuries, and provided a suitable place for the ladies of the house to walk indoors, as well as for displaying family portraits and other pictures.

The addition of the long gallery meant that a paved quadrangle was formed, to be known as 'The Court of Sovereigns'. There is a doorway in the centre of each of the surrounding walls of this courtyard, above each of which are ornamental niches containing small statues of Henry VIII and his three 'sovereign' children respectively. These were placed here in 1617. The four walls around the courtyard are of sandstone and flint arranged in a chequered pattern.

Robert Haydon died in 1626, and left Cadhay to his eldest son, Gideon (1609–1680). He married Margaret, the daughter of John Davie of Sandford, near Crediton, by whom he had seven sons and five daughters. During the next 120 years Cadhay was to be owned by a succession of Gideon Haydons, the property passing from father to son.

Gideon the second was the third son of the first Gideon and his wife, Margaret, and he inherited Cadhay on his father's death. He married Eleanor by whom he had three sons. By their marriage settlement dated 28 January 1660/61, Cadhay, together with other lands in Devon, was held in trust for this second Gideon during his life, and the estates would then pass to his son, also named Gideon.

The second Gideon died at Ottery St Mary in August 1680, and so the third generation of that name succeeded to Cadhay. He was married to Catherine, the daughter of John Stoakes of London.

Although the Haydons were a wealthy family, they were also very extravagant, and spent considerable sums of money on celebrating the restoration of Charles II. Continual lavish spending was to lead to financial difficulties, and the various estates, including Cadhay, had to be mortgaged. Trustees were appointed to hold certain property for the fourth Gideon on his marriage in 1693 to Alice, the daughter of John Fitch of Henbury in Dorset. But in addition to the heavy mortgages, the third Gideon Haydon and his son were burdened with debts amounting to £17,000. It was inevitable that some of the property had to be sold to pay off the debts.

Because of disputes within the family, Chancery proceedings were commenced in 1698 by the fourth Gideon against his father (the third Gideon), and the trustees.

The fifth Gideon Haydon married Anne Hanbury, a widow, in 1773 and, having advanced money to her husband to help him to discharge his debts, she was later to accuse him of using this for stocking his estate! Although efforts were made to save Cadhay for Alice, widow of the fourth Gideon, and her son, they were of no avail. In 1736 Cadhay and all that remained of the estate had to be put on the market for the first time in its history in order to clear the mounting debts. The unforunate Anne, wife of the fifth Gideon, lost her marriage portion on the sale of the property, and succeeded in recovering only £190 of the arrears of her annuity.

Cadhay was bought by John Brown of Richmond, Surrey, for £5,800. After residing there for only a year, within which short time he was made an assistant governor of the church, he sold the estate to William Peere Williams for £6,750, making what in those days was considered to be a substantial profit. Peere Williams was the second son of an eminent lawyer, the editor of *Chancery Reports* in three volumes (1695–1736).

Cadhay had fallen into a sad state of disrepair, and the new owner was soon to make extensive alterations. The north front or entrance was refaced with Beer stone, and the great Tudor windows were replaced with two rows of sash windows, a recent innovation. The chimney stacks, however, were retained in their original form, but Peere Williams had otherwise updated the north entrance in Georgian classical style. This work was carried out about 1740.

The great hall, which rose to its splendid timber roof, was divided horizontally into two, by constructing a floor and ceiling. The fine Tudor fireplace was plastered over, but this was fortunately restored to its original state many years later (1910). Peere Williams imposed upon Cadhay much that was typically Georgian in character, and this is to be observed, in particular in the drawing room.

He became a governor of the church in 1745, and was chairman when the Rev. John Coleridge was appointed Master of the King's School in August 1760, to be followed by his appointment as vicar of Ottery St Mary by the end of that same year. But Peere Williams appears to have been a somewhat difficult man, and was often at loggerheads with his fellow governors, notably Richard Copplestone, over the filling of vacancies. In 1758 application was made to the King's Bench, and eventually the court upheld his conduct as being very reasonable.

On the death of William Peere Williams in 1766, without male issue, Cadhay passed to his nephew, Sir Booth Williams. He agreed to sell the property to his uncle's widow, Elizabeth, and to effect this a special Act of Parliament was passed in 1771. Mrs. Peere Williams continued to live at Cadhay until her death in 1792 and, as her elder daughter, Anne, had pre-deceased her, the estate passed to the younger daughter, Elizabeth, who had on 22 June 1771 married Admiral Thomas Graves of Thanks in Cornwall. He became a vice-admiral, and in 1794 was created Lord Graves in recognition of his services as second-in-command to Lord Howe at the great naval victory off Ushant on the 'Glorious First of June'. He died at Cadhay in 1802.

His daughter, Elizabeth Anne Graves, married William Bagwell of Ashcott, Somerset, but died within two months of her marriage. In 1803 her younger sister, Anne Elizabeth Graves, was married to Sir Thomas Hare, Bart., of Stow Bardolf in Norfolk, but they never lived at Cadhay. They decided to let off the adjoining farm, and divide the house, so that the tenant-farmer occupied the west side and the east side was let as a private residence.[4]

With the constant threat of invasion during the Napoleonic wars, temporary barracks were built in 1803 to the west of the town. The master of the barracks, Mr. Palmer, became tenant of the private house or east part of Cadhay. The barracks were dismantled in 1814, and some years later Captain Collins, a sea captain, became tenant. His widow was still in occupation in 1909, when the estate was sold by Sir Thomas Hare's grandson, Sir Ralph Hare, to W. C. Dampier Whetham.

During the 19th century Cadhay had become much neglected, possibly due to having absentee landlords in Norfolk, and the new owner was faced with a formidable task in carrying out repair work. He was responsible for making some much desired alterations, and restoring Cadhay as nearly as possible to something of its former Tudor beauty. The farmhouse, known as Cadhay Barton, was built for occupation by the tenant-farmer, and cottages and farm buildings were added to the estate.

Although W. C. Dampier Whetham made extensive improvements to Cadhay in excellent taste during 1911 and most of 1912, he did not remain long, and the house was again let separately. In 1924, Major Barton N. W. William-Powlett became tenant, and it was by a strange coincidence that he should have been descended from another branch of the family of Sir Amyas Poulett, whose daughter had been mistress of Cadhay in the days of its Elizabethan greatness. Fortunately, as sitting tenant, he was able to purchase the entire property in 1935, and his family have resided there since. He died in 1953 and Cadhay passed to his eldest son, Captain Newton J. W. William-Powlett, D.S.C., R.N. In 1956 a government grant, arranged through the Historic Buildings Council for England, enabled urgent repairs to be carried out on the north side of the house, and to some of the chimneys. Captain Newton William-Powlett was chairman of Ottery Church Corporation from 1958 until 1962, and so followed in the footsteps of John Haydon.

On the death of Captain William-Powlett in November 1963, his only son, Mr. Oliver N. W. William-Powlett, succeeded to the estate, which he farms. He also has become a church governor.

As seen today, Cadhay is a courtyard manor house of mixed Tudor and Georgian architecture. The original Elizabethan part of the house is best viewed from the east across the fields. Here, backed by the wooded farmlands of West Hill, John Haydon's 'fair new house' again reflects much of the true spirit of Tudor England.

The Chanter's House

As we have already seen in Chapter Four, the chanter, or precentor, was one of the senior canons of the collegiate church. He resided at the Chanter's House, and was responsible for leading the singing during divine service.

On the dissolution of the college in 1545, the manor of Ottery, which included the medieval Chanter's House, was granted by Henry VIII to Edward Seymour, Earl of Hertford who, in the next reign, became the Protector Somerset. In 1548, he granted a lease of 'Le Chaunter's House' to Richard Duke of Otterton but, on the attainder of Somerset four years later, the manor of Ottery reverted to the crown.

By 1561, the lease had been surrendered, and the crown then granted a new lease to John Courtenay of Powderham and his son, Roger, for their lives. John Courtenay was a younger son of Sir William Courtenay, who was a member of that junior branch of the family which was eventually to succeed to the earldom of Devon. Roger Courtenay died insolvent in 1599, and the crown had to distrain on his best beast in order to recover the arrears of rent.

In 1617 a 99-year lease of the manor was granted to Sir Francis Bacon and others. But in 1628 this lease and the freehold reversion were purchased by Robert Collins. On his death in the following year, the estate passed to his son, also named Robert, who supported the parliamentarians during the English Civil War, and entertained Sir Thomas Fairfax at the Chanter's House in autumn 1645 (*see* Chapter Seven). It was here that Oliver Cromwell met Fairfax to discuss the future campaign in the West, which led to the surrender of Exeter in the following spring. The oak-panelled room in which this convocation was held is now the dining room of the Chanter's House, and a plaque on the door records that:

> In this Convention Room Oliver Cromwell in the fall of the year 1645 convened the people of the town and neighbourhood and demanded of them men and money for the Civil War.

Robert Collins died in 1653, and it is stated in the parish register that he was 'one of ye ffower Governors' of the church. He was succeeded by his son, the third Robert, who, as a fellow of Exeter College, Oxford, took holy orders in 1652 and became chaplain to his college. He was later to be vicar of Talaton and, as shown in Chapter Seven, his recusancy caused him to suffer bitter religious persecution amid some lively times. This eventually forced him and his family to seek religious freedom in Holland. The Chanter's House was sold in 1685 to Thomas Heath, a member of a well-known Exeter family. The house was re-named Heath's Court, after its new owner, and was to be known by this name for over 200 years.

Thomas Heath was succeeded by his son, Staplehill Heath, who married Ann Duke of Otterton. They had a son, John. Ann died in 1734, and Staplehill Heath then married Elizabeth Bartlett, a widow, who survived him, and died at Heath's Court in 1786 at the advanced age of 112 years. She could remember the landing of Prince William of Orange at Torbay in November 1688, and that he had dined at Ottery St Mary on his journey to London to take the crown from James II. Staplehill Heath had died in 1759, and his son, John, succeeded him. He assumed the name of Duke when he inherited through his mother the Duke estates at Otterton.

Colonel James Coleridge, the eldest surviving son of the Rev. John Coleridge, had been living at Tiverton, but on 19 October 1796 he purchased Heath's Court, and the property has remained in the ownership of his descendants since that date. He married Frances Taylor, who through her mother was a co-heiress of the Duke family of Otterton. She had come to stay with her maiden aunts, Sara and

Ann Duke at The Priory, and it was there that she met James Coleridge. They were married in 1788 at the church of St Mary Arches in Exeter, where James's father and mother had been married 35 years before.

Writing of him in 1797, his youngest brother, the poet, said:

> My third brother, James, has been in the army since the age of sixteen, has married a woman of fortune, and now lives at Ottery St Mary, a respectable man.

The colonel became a local magistrate, and in a letter dated January 1820 to his son, John Taylor Coleridge, who was at the start of a brilliant legal career, he wrote:

> I have been attacking the idle Rascals of ye Town [Ottery St Mary] . . . and this week I have sent a lot of eight to the Stocks for being drunk in Bear Bastyn's house on a Sunday, unless they pay five shillings [25p] each and ye expenses.

He died at Heath's Court (now the Chanter's House) early in January 1836, aged 76 years, and was laid to rest in the north aisle of the church.

Mention has already been made of his second son, Sir John Taylor Coleridge, P.C., D.C.L., a judge of the Queen's Bench, in Chapters Six and Ten. In August 1846 he headed a committee which launched an appeal to raise a fund for the reseating and, if possible, the entire restoration of the interior of the church 'to its original beauty'. He undertook to restore the Dorset aisle at his own expense, and was largely responsible for the extensive restoration of the church, which was carried out under William Butterfield during 1849–50.

His eldest son was John Duke Coleridge, of whom brief mention was made in the last chapter. He was born on 3 December 1820 and, after going to Eton, he went to Oxford, where he became a scholar of Balliol. He was called to the Bar, and entered upon an outstanding legal career. His fellow barristers on the Western Circuit called him 'good John', for he was tall and graceful with classic features, and his voice possessed a musical beauty.

Entering parliament, he became in turn Solicitor-General, and then Attorney-General. On his appointment as Chief Justice of Common Pleas (as it was then) in December 1873, he was created first Baron Coleridge. As from 1875 he became Lord Chief Justice of England.

When Solicitor-General he led for the defence in the famous Titchborne case in 1871 in which a fat butcher from Wagga Wagga in New South Wales, Australia, claimed to be the long-lost heir to the Titchborne family estates in Hampshire. The case lasted 102 days.

As Lord Chief Justice, Lord Coleridge tried the sensational Baccarat case in which the Prince of Wales (later King Edward VII) gave evidence. This case concerned a Victorian scandal over alleged cheating at cards at a house party at Tanby Croft, near Hull, and aroused wide interest in 1891, largely due to the painful disclosure of corruption in society.

Although much of his time had to be spent living in London, Lord Coleridge came to his beloved family home at Ottery St Mary whenever his duties permitted. In 1883 Heath's Court was considerably enlarged and a splendid library was added overlooking the peaceful parkland to the west of the house. The oak beams of the original hall were preserved.

Lord Coleridge died on 14 June 1894 and, after an impressive service in Westminster Abbey, his remains were brought to Ottery St Mary for his funeral there the following day. He was laid to rest in the family vault in the churchyard.

He was succeeded by his eldest son, Bernard John Seymour Coleridge, born in 1851, who also became a distinguished High Court judge (Plate 22). He wrote *The Story of a Devonshire House,* in which he gave an affectionate account of members of the Coleridge family.

The Chanter's House, with its historic associations, although much altered in Victoria's reign, remains the home of the present Lord and Lady Coleridge.

Escot House

The name is first recorded as 'Estcot' in 1227, and means 'the western manor'. Early in the Stuart period the estate belonged to the Channon family and, as mentioned in Chapter Seven, Elizabeth Channon, the only daughter and heiress of Richard Channon of Escot, married the Rev. Melchizedeck Alford, who was vicar of Ottery St Mary. In 1680 her husband joined with her and their two daughters in conveying Escot to Sir Walter Yonge, who had entertained James, Duke of Monmouth, at the Great House, Colyton, in August of that year.

Shortly after purchasing the estate, Sir Walter Yonge began building a mansion there, which was not completed until about 1688. We learn that this house was built of brick with stone ornamentation, and was almost square, having a frontage of 90 feet. There were 15 rooms in the basement, and 16 on the ground floor. The bedrooms were 14 feet in height, and in addition there were 16 attic rooms.

Some of the workmen engaged on the building are believed to have rallied to the support of Monmouth when he landed at Lyme Regis in 1685, and they fought at Sedgemoor. They were taken prisoners and sentenced at Exeter Assizes by the infamous Judge Jeffreys. It was ordered that they should be hanged on a gibbet erected at four cross roads to the east of Talaton, which has ever since been known by the name of Bittery Cross.

On 13 August 1789 Sir George Yonge, who then owned Escot, entertained King George III, Queen Charlotte and three of the princesses when on their way from Weymouth to Exeter. The royal party was given a loyal welcome by a great crowd which assembled at the entrance to the estate.

The Yonge family lived at Escot until 1794, when Sir George Yonge, who was Secretary for War, sold the property, which comprised of 4,000 acres, to Sir John Kennaway. He was a younger son of William Kennaway, an Exeter serge-maker, who had in 1743 founded the business of a wine merchant in that city. John was a successful diplomat in the East India Company, and was created a baronet in 1791.

The house was completely destroyed by fire on 28 December 1808 with the loss of all the elegant furniture, and most of the valuable paintings. This disaster was caused by the curtains in a dressing room ('the chintze room') being set on fire by a lighted candle which had been left there whilst the family were entertaining guests at dinner. Although the property was uninsured, Sir John Kennaway accepted his grievous loss with commendable fortitude.

It was not until nearly 30 years later that a new house was built, the first stone being laid by his infant grandson, John Henry Kennaway, on 6 September 1837. The house stands in beautiful wooded parkland ornamented with its clumps of beech, and a lake. In *Pendennis,* W. M. Thackeray tells of the hollow tree in the park in which the young lovers deposited their letters, and the 'Fairoaks' of this novel may well have been at Escot, which Thackeray knew well.

Sir John Kennaway died in 1836 and was succeeded by his son, also named John. It was he who was responsible for building the little church of St Philip and St James in 1837–8 at a cost of about £3,000, and Escot became a separate parish two years later. The church is in the Early English style with a turret and bell.

In 1873 John Henry Kennaway, who had laid that first stone of Escot House nearly 36 years before, succeeded to the estate as the third baronet.

Although the passing years have brought about many changes, the Kennaways are still the owners of Escot and its lovely park.

Holcombe

The ancient mansion house of Holcombe (pronounced 'Hokum') was situate on the east of the parish, and stood in a hollow (or deep) combe from which it took its name.[5] This sub-manor comprised 346 acres of farmland on the lower slopes of East Hill, and had a private chapel, dedicated to St Leonard, which Thomas de Brantyngham, Bishop of Exeter (1370–95), licensed on 13 June 1388.[6]

Holcombe appears to have originally belonged to the family of Malherbe. Towards the end of Henry VI's reign the property passed to John Moore, who resided there, and the estate remained in the occupation of his family for the next 100 years.

In 1550 John Evelegh (1511–1586), a local magistrate, bought the property from Hugh Moore, together with other lands in South Devon. He became M.P. for Tavistock and Totnes in 1554. By his second wife, Joan Southcot of Bovey Tracey, who died in 1594, he had 11 children of whom the eldest, George, succeeded to Holcombe. His youngest daughter, Joan (born in 1567), married Richard Sherman of Knightstone (q.v.) John Evelegh died in October 1586 intestate, and letters of administration to his estate were granted to his widow, Joan, and his eldest son, George, who was an ardent catholic.

A warrant was issued in 1605 to search the houses of George Evelegh and Thomas Babington of Ottery St Mary 'upon credible information of the great resort made to them in the night season and other unlawful times of Recusants, Papists, and other persons ill-affected to his Majesty'.

George Evelegh died at Holcombe in 1632. As his son, George, had predeceased him, he left the estate to his grandson, also named George (1618–1689), who became a captain in the royalist troop during the Civil War, and was later punished for supporting King Charles I. Two-thirds of his estates were taken from him by Cromwell.

Commissioners for compounding, as they were called, were sent into all counties to collect evidence of recusancy:

> 1650 Feb. 14th. Ottery St. Mary. Jo. Serle and Richard Clapp to the Commissioners:
>
> We send you enclosed a discovery of a considerable sume of money due unto Capt. George Evelegh, a Papist in armes, wherein we suppose the Commonwealth to have an interest.

In 1649 George Evelegh had sold Holcombe to Humphrey Walround of Ash, near Fenny Bridges, although the purchase money was not actually paid until 1653. However, his cousin, Gilbert Evelegh (1604–71), of Totnes, who was a grandson of John Evelegh the founder of the family fortunes, bought back Holcombe from Humphrey Walround. He was thrice mayor of Totnes, in 1654, 1663, and 1671, and, like his grandfather, he became M.P. for that town. As his only son George had died in infancy (1640), he left his estate by will to a distant cousin, William Evelegh of Talaton, and Holcombe passed to him in 1672.

But this branch of the family came to an end with co-heiresses Anne and Judith. Judith, who married Sir William Drake of Ashe, near Axminster, died in 1701. Her elder sister, Anne Evelegh, married, first Thomas Hobbs, and after his death, John Leigh in 1694. On her death in 1719, Holcombe passed to the Leighs, and remained in that family until 1797.

It was not until after this date that the modern spelling of the name of 'Eveleigh' was adopted by the family. The fine old manor house was destroyed by fire, and all that remains today are traces of the foundations near the Georgian house known as Holcombe Barton.

Knightstone

A mile to the south of Ottery St Mary, the medieval manor house of Knightstone lies across a small green valley through which a stream makes its way towards the river Otter. The name would appear to be derived from the family of le Knight, and is shown in the earliest records as 'Cnizteston' (1284) and as 'Knyghtiston' (1330), meaning 'the knight's tūn [farmstead]'.

According to Tristram Risdon's *Survey of the County of Devon* 'about 44 Edward III [1372] Richard, son of John de Knightston, conveyed this land to Thomas Bittlesgate, who made his dwelling there'. Bittlesgate is believed to have been responsible for building the great hall, which is 26ft. long by 20ft. in breadth, and was later flanked by gabled wings. On 16 October 1381 Thomas de Brantyngham, Bishop of Exeter (1370–94), granted a licence to Bittlesgate and his wife, Jane, to build a private chapel. This licence in Latin reads:

> Oratoria sive Capellas infra maneria sau de
> Kyngeston infra parochiam de Otry Sancte Marie . . .

By his will Thomas Bittlesgate devised Knightstone to his descendants in tail with remainder to William, Lord Bonville of Shute, near Colyton, on failure of issue of the Bittlesgate family.

In 1494, on the death of Richard Bittlesgate without issue, the estate passed by entail to Lord Bonville's great-granddaughter and heiress, Lady Cicely Grey, Marchioness of Dorset, to whom reference has already been made in Chapter Four.[7] She died in 1530 in her 70th year, and left her estate, including 'Knightstone' and her other manors, to her eldest son, Thomas Grey, 2nd Marquess of Dorset, and his heirs for 'such an estate of inheritance as to me dissendyd'.

Knightstone merged in the estates of the Marquesses of Dorset until 1553. When Henry Grey, Earl of Suffolk, the grandson of Lady Cicely, attempted to place his daughter, Lady Jane Grey, upon the throne, this resulted in his attainder and execution.[8] His estates were forfeited, and Knightstone lapsed to the crown.

William Sherman, a wealthy merchant of Ottery St Mary, purchased the property in 1554, and the stone fireplace in the hall was built by him in 1567. The large mullioned windows were added about this time. He founded almshouses in Yonder Street, Ottery St Mary, and these are now represented by 12 flats for elderly people, known as Sherman House in recognition of this benefaction (*see* Chapter Twelve).

On the death of William Sherman in 1583, Knightstone passed to his son, John Sherman, whose second wife was Margaret, the daughter of Sir Bernard Drake of Ashe, near Musbury. Tragically, John Sherman and his elder son, Richard, were both drowned on the same day in 1617, as their epitaph in St Stephen's chapel in Ottery church records:

> And then one month, one very day,
> Took both the Sire and Son away.

His second son, Gideon Sherman, succeeded to Knightstone. He married Anne, the daughter of Nicholas Fry of Yarty, near Axminster, in 1618, but she died in the first week of her marriage. This sad event is also recorded in an epitaph in St Stephen's chapel:

> No sooner was she to a loving mate
> From careful parents solemnly bequeath'd,
> The new alliance, scarce congratulate,
> But she from him, them, all, was straight bereav'd;
> Slipping from bridal feast to funeral bere,
> She soon fell sick, expired; lies buried here.

The poet Robert Southey, during a visit to Ottery St Mary with his friend Samuel Taylor Coleridge in September 1799, was of the opinion that these interesting epitaphs to members of the Sherman family were composed by William Browne (1588–1645), as their feeling and style were in keeping with his known work (*see* Chapter Seven).

On a floor slab in front of St Stephen's chapel are three monumental brasses, depicting William Sherman, his father, John Sherman, and his son, Richard. One bar has gone, but the remaining two are inscribed: 'Ioannes ob. 1542', and 'Gvilielmus ob. 1583'.

Gideon Sherman re-married in 1618, his second wife being a Coplestone. It was possibly about this date that the 14th-century roof of the hall was covered with an ornamental plaster barrel-vaulted ceiling, which later collapsed, leaving only the Jacobean plaster frieze, which remains to this day.

On the death of Gideon Sherman without issue in 1627, Knightstone passed to his widow.

In 1714 Elizabeth Coplestone gave some communion plate to Ottery church. This consisted of two large silver flagons bearing the arms of Coplestone quartered with those of Drake of Ashe, and each being inscribed 'The gift of Eliz., relict of Richard Coplestone, Esq., of Knightstone in this parish, 1714', and also two silver chalices bearing the same arms. All these items were made by John Elston of Exeter.

John Coplestone, the last of the family, died in 1759, and his widow married a Hawtrey, whose family was connected with Eton College. Dr. Joseph Drury, headmaster of Harrow, bought Knightstone from Stephen Hawtrey's trustees in 1803, and retired to Devon two years later. His son, the Rev. Charles Drury, carried out much-needed restoration to the hall and the adjoining rooms in 1837, as it had been used for farm purposes, and some of the windows were blocked up. He left the property by will to his great-nephew, Gerald Drury, whose father had been chaplain to the House of Commons. From him the estate passed to Saxon Drury, and was conveyed by him to Matthew Ellis in 1886. His son, Matthew William Ellis, succeeded to Knightstone in 1913, and farmed the land until March 1941, when the estate was sold to the late Lieutenant-Colonel Reginald Cooper.

He accepted the restoration of this historic house as a challenge and set about its re-discovery, carrying out extensive works in careful detail and excellent taste, to preserve the true character of the property. By the skilful use of yew hedges to form compartments, he laid out the ornamental gardens in a delightful manner.

On his death, Knightstone once more came into the market, and was bought by Mr. Geoffrey Robinson who, during his 15 years' ownership, made considerable further improvements. He died in February 1982. This attractive house in its peaceful setting has been preserved with devoted care through the centuries, but never more so than by its recent owners.

The Manor House

The word 'manor' is derived from the French 'manoir', meaning 'habitation', and was introduced by William the Conqueror's commissioners when making the Domesday Survey (1086). It originally referred to the dwelling or residence of the lord or baron, but in time came to mean the manor house, the home farm or the lord's demesne, including the surrounding tenant farmsteads, which, together with the church, formed the typical feudal grouping.

The original manor hall at 'Otrei' was possibly built towards the end of the 12th century as there is some evidence of the existence of a small church here by that time (*see* Chapter Three), which would have been an appendage to the manor. When John de Grandisson founded his college of canons, the manor hall was incorporated with the collegiate buildings. It was·here that the manorial courts were held, and all the secular business of the estate conducted. The canons of the college became the new lords of the manor.

On the dissolution of the college in 1545, Henry VIII granted the manor to Edward Seymour, Earl of Hertford, who later became Protector Somerset. When he was attainted for high treason in 1552, the manor passed by forfeiture to the Crown where it remained until sold early in the reign of Charles I. For a short time it had been held by Henry, Prince of Wales, the elder brother of Charles, and during this period it was farmed by three responsible tenants, with a high steward and his deputy in charge. But Prince Henry had died in 1612 while still a minor.

In 1639 the remainder of a 99-year lease of the manor was purchased by John Ledgingham. On his death in 1654, he was succeeded as lord of the manor by his son, Warwick Ledgingham, who appears to have been a very litigious person, constantly at cross-purposes with his tenants.

The lords of the manor were closely associated with the church, and it was usual for the manor house to be situated on the north side of it. The north porch of the church was reserved for the use of the lord of the manor and his family. The manor hall was open to the rafters, but in the course of time various additions were made, mainly at right-angles to the original building, and so it became a house within the modern meaning.

Incident to the manor were two courts, which were held twice each year on what were known as 'law days', and the tenants were required to attend at the manor hall. The functions of these manorial courts have already been explained in Chapter Eight.

In October 1822 the manor was conveyed to Sir John Kennaway, Bart., of Escot, whereupon he became lord of the manor, and his family continued as such until recent times.

The manor house was later purchased by Francis George Coleridge, a nephew of the poet, who practised as a solicitor in the town, and died there in 1854 (*see* Chapter Ten).

The original manor hall, where the courts had been held since feudal times, was pulled down in 1860, but traces of this building remain. The house was later to become the residence of Mary Frances Keble Coleridge, a younger sister of the first Baron Coleridge. During the next 100 years it was let to a series of tenants, some of whom, prior to 1901, enjoyed the private garden and fish-ponds, since replaced by the extension to the old churchyard. Although the manor hall has gone, this quiet corner in the shadow of the church preserves memories of an historic past.

The Cokes of Thorne

The Coke or Cooke family lived at the ancient mansion of Thorne, lying beyond the river Otter to the west of the town. In King John's reign (1199–1216), the property was held by John Thorne, and in the time of Edward III (1327–1377), it belonged to Roger Thorne. On his death, without issue, the estate passed to his sister, Jane, who had married Henry Cooke. Her husband survived her, and succeeded to Thorne. Richard Coke was born in 1607, and the property remained in the Coke family until his death, without issue. The estate was then sold, and passed into other hands.

Families tended to remain in their immediate neighbourhood, and consequently there was considerable intermarriage. The leading families of Ottery St Mary and the surrounding district, during late Tudor and early Stuart times, were the Haydons of Cadhay, the Cokes of Thorne, the Shermans of Knightstone, the Eveleghs of Holcombe, the Collins of the Chanter's House, the Drakes of Musbury, the Waldrons of Ash, and the Coplestones, who hailed from the Crediton area.

John Coke was born in 1589. He married Margaret, the daughter of Richard Sherman of Knightstone, on 14 May 1607. He became an assistant governor of Ottery church in 1625, and continued to serve until his death on 28 March 1632 at the age of forty-two. His son, John, who lived at St Erme, north-east of Truro in Cornwall, was married to Johanna Haydon on 13 June 1629.

The monument in the Dorset aisle of Ottery church contains a life-sized figure of John Coke in armour, standing rather awkwardly beneath a heavy classical canopy. It was, perhaps, because he was in armour and holding a sword that he is often referred to as 'Captain Coke' by the local people. The gruesome skull set in the wall below the monument is the classical emblem of death.

It is an awesome and rather gloomy memorial in a dark corner of the aisle, and this may have given rise to certain strange tales. It is said that at midnight on New Year's Eve John Coke steps down from his monument and walks around the church. Another story relates how he is supposed to have killed his brother accidentally with his sword, but these are local tales befitting a melancholy effigy. In 1726, his grandson was responsible for having the memorial carefully restored.

Chapter Twelve

THE END OF AN ERA

Early Twentieth Century

WITH THE DAWN of a new century the Victorian age closed at the death of the old queen on 22 January 1901. She had been in failing health for several years, but had been spared to attain her Diamond Jubilee in 1897, and her reign had lasted longer than that of any other British monarch.

The 19th century had, however, closed with a revival of the Boer War which clouded the last years of the queen's reign. Kruger attacked Cape Colony and Natal, and when Mafeking was eventually relieved on 18 May 1900, after a siege lasting 217 days, there were wild rejoicings throughout the country. At Ottery St Mary the local tradesmen gathered in Broad Street, firing guns in rapid succession to the accompaniment of the cheers of a jubilant crowd. A soup kitchen had been set up at the rear of a butcher's shop, and had attracted people from all parts of the town who came with their bowls for the welcome hot soup. When the war ended two years later, the people of Ottery St Mary presented gold watches to each of the local volunteers.

The advent of the motor car was to bring about a change in the lifestyle of the country. With easier means of transport there was a steady drift of population from the country districts to the larger towns, and even overseas. The population of Ottery St Mary had been 4,421 in 1851, but by the end of the century it had fallen by nearly a thousand, whilst that of Exeter had risen by more than 14,000 during that same period.

The dusty streets in summer were watered by a water-cart, a galvanised tank drawn by a horse. The tank was filled from the stream below the churchyard wall, and it was usual to find a number of children running behind, washing their hands in the spraying water.

The churchyard was extended to include the area formerly the garden and site of the Great House (*see* Chapter Eight). This ground was consecrated on 23 February 1901, but burials were not made there until 1903/04.

During 1908/09 the spire on the north tower of the church was completely dismantled, and a new wooden framework was erected. Most of the old lead was used again.

When the ancient weathercock was brought down it was found that the tail bore several holes which, as mentioned in Chapter Seven, had possibly been caused by musket shot during the Civil War. This tail had to be replaced by a replica.

Not until May 1977 was the weathercock again taken down, on this occasion for regilding.

In the early days of this century the cattle markets were great occasions, especially the Christmas market. They were held partly in The Flexton, and sheep were penned in hurdles along the length of The College. Cattle and sheep were also sold in Broad Street, where part of the market took place until 1913, when it was moved to a site near St Saviour's bridge. Markets were held there on the first and third Mondays in each month, but were sadly discontinued in the late 1950s.

The Old Ottregians Society

One Sunday afternoon in 1898 six young men from Ottery St Mary, who were then living in London, met on the steps of St Paul's Cathedral, and resolved to form a Society to promote good fellowship among Ottery people wherever they might be. And so was founded the Old Ottregians Society, which took as its motto 'Floreat Ottregia' ('May Ottery Flourish'). It soon became a very active society, and from 1907 trips were arranged from London (Waterloo Station) on Whit Monday, the return rail fare being 6s. 6d. (33p). There was an occasion when nearly 1,000 members made the journey to Ottery St Mary in two special trains, arriving at 6 a.m. and leaving at 6 p.m.

The headquarters of the Society were in London, and at a meeting held on 11 December 1910, 'The Ottery Song', which had been specially composed by Bernard, Lord Coleridge, was sung for the first time.

> There is a place, dear native place!
>   Amid the meadows fair,
> Between the hills, beside the stream,
>   Where blows the soft light air.
>
> *Chorus:* O! Ottery dear! O! Ottery fair!
>   My heart goes out to thee,
> Thou art my home, where'er I roam,
>   The West! the West for me!
>
> Sweet-breathing kine, the old grey church,
>   The curfew tolling slow,
> The glory of the Western sky,
>   The warm red earth below.
>
> *Chorus:* O! Ottery dear! etc.
>
> The whistling Cock, the tumbling weir,
>   The cave where Pixies dwell,
> The sweet old place which gave us birth
>   We know—we love it well.
>
> *Chorus:* O! Ottery dear! etc.

> Then let us clasp each other's hands,
> Our Childhood's love renew,
> We stand together round the World,
> For Ottery hearts are true!

Chorus: O! Ottery dear! etc.

Although the melody lingers on when the old carillon chimes in the church tower, it is sad to record that such a splendid society as the Old Ottregians was disbanded in 1948, following the death of Sidney Herbert Godfrey, who had been for 50 years the enthusiastic honorary secretary. His love and loyalty to his native place will long be remembered.

World War I

Old traditions and ideas were to be so severely shaken by the onslaught of the First World War that life could never be the same. Times were changing rapidly, and people were preparing to meet the challenge of a different world.

Germany's rising naval power had for some years been presenting an ominous threat to world peace, and storm clouds were gathering rapidly. The joys of that beautiful but uneasy summer of 1914 were abruptly shattered on Tuesday, 4 August, when war was declared against a belligerent Germany, and the world, as it had been known, was lost for ever. Yet there were many who expected that the war would be over by Christmas that year!

Young men from Ottery St Mary left their homes in answer to their country's call, and local women soon rallied to their support by organising committees to send warm clothing and food parcels to their menfolk fighting on the western front. Sphagnum moss was gathered at West Hill for use in medical dressings.

News was anxiously awaited, and before long it seemed as if the war would never end as the relentless struggle in Flanders' mud went on month after month with mounting losses. By 1917 there were severe shortages of food as the German U-boat campaign tightened its grip in an effort to force Britain into submission by starvation. Food prices had risen alarmingly during the past three years.

The opposing lines of the western front swayed to and fro with little or no gains being made during four terrible years until, in the autumn of 1918, the tide at last turned in favour of the allies. On the morning of Monday, 11 November, came the news that an armistice had been signed, and hostilities ceased at 11 o'clock.

The townspeople assembled to celebrate the peace with a large bonfire in the middle of Broad Street, and flags were hung from first-floor windows along the streets. Then, on 6 July of the following year, there was a peace thanksgiving in which the town silver band took a prominent part.

Of those men who had gone from Ottery to serve their country, there were many who did not return. In addition to those who had been seriously wounded, the Devonshire Regiment lost nearly 6,000 men in the bitter conflict.

Prince of Wales's visit in 1921

On Tuesday, 17 May 1921, the Prince of Wales (later to become Edward VIII) came to Ottery St Mary. When the royal car reached Broad Street, the prince got out and greeted the large crowd which had gathered there to welcome him. He was at that time staying at Bicton as the guest of Lord Clinton, and his grandfather, King Edward VII, had been a frequent visitor to Bicton in the early part of the century.

The Prince of Wales was extremely popular and, during those years shortly after the First World War, was rapturously referred to as 'Our Prince Charming'. During his brief visit to the town the King's School Cadet Corps formed a guard of honour.

The dark 'thirties

The early 1930s were gloomily overshadowed by the spectre of increasing unemployment throughout the country. Ottery St Mary, because of its proximity to Exeter, Devon's county town, was not as seriously affected as some places. In North Devon the position had become extremely grave, and the towns of Bideford, Torrington and Barnstaple were declining. Farming, in particular, was facing a severe depression, largely due to foreign competition, and there was a steady drift in population towards the towns in search of employment.

In 1935 the silver jubilee of King George V brought some relief in an otherwise cheerless period, and two years later Ottery St Mary celebrated the coronation of King George VI and Queen Elizabeth in a flag-bedecked Broad Street, with a gaily festooned pole erected in the middle of the street to support the fluttering bunting.

When economic conditions began to show signs of recovery towards the end of the decade, the menace of Nazi Germany loomed like an ominous cloud as Adolf Hitler threatened the peace of Europe with his wild rantings.

World War II

On Saturday, 2 September 1939, the first evacuees arrived at Ottery St Mary from a London school. Each child was carefully labelled, and carried a small bundle of possessions; they had been swept off suddenly to face a very different way of life in the comparative safety of the South-West. War was declared against Germany the next day.

Although no bombs had fallen on Devon during the First World War, it was to be a different story this time, for the civilian population was to suffer severely. Plymouth and Exeter were ruthlessly attacked from the air, and bombs were indiscriminately dropped by the German raiders over other parts of the county. In Exeter 80 people were killed, over 100 suffered injuries, and much of the city was reduced to ruins. Although no actual damage was caused to Ottery St Mary, several bombs fell in the vicinity. German planes passed overhead on their way to devastating raids on Cardiff and other parts of South Wales, and also on the West Midlands.

Further names were added to those who had been killed during World War I— such is the cost and beastliness of war. Among the dead were 21 old boys of King's School.

When the war ended in 1945, after nearly six dreadful years, there were general rejoicings, and the church bells of St Mary, Ottery, rang out again after their long silence. These eight bells in the south tower were shortly afterwards recast by John Taylor and Company of Loughborough, and hung in a new frame. On 29 October 1949 'the poor man's only music' pealed out once more across the Devon countryside.

Some anniversaries

During those war years there had been a steady increase in the number of pupils at the King's School and, although the 400th anniversary of its foundation was reached in 1945, it was decided to defer any public celebration of this quater centenary to a more opportune moment.

In the late 1960s and the early 1970s came the commemoration of further anniversaries. A special service was held on 5 December 1969 to mark the 600th anniversary of the consecration of the church (or some part thereof) by Bishop Walter Bronescombe, at which the late Dr. Robert C. Mortimer, Bishop of Exeter (1949–73) preached the sermon. Then in the following year the centenary of the founding of Ottery Hospital was celebrated, and a handsome clock for the entrance hall was presented to mark the occasion.

On 22 October 1972, a commemoration service was held in the church on the bicentenary of the birth of Devon's literary genius, Samuel Taylor Coleridge, and a moving sermon was delivered by his great-great-grandson, the late Rev. Nicholas Coleridege.

Industry

During those far-off days of the mid–19th century, the owner of the silk factory had been Thomas A. Newberry, who combined silk manufacture there with his business of a corn-miller at the adjoining town mill. But towards the end of the century the silk industry had declined, and in 1896 both the factory and the town mill were sold.

Early in the 1900s this Georgian factory was for a time used as a bottling plant for mineral waters, and then followed various other uses, including the manufacture of brushes, paper-bags, collars and shirts, and also letterpress and copper-plate printing. In World War II the building was taken over by the War Department, and used as a store, and for billeting troops. Flour had continued to be ground at the town mill until 1937, when the last miller, William J. Digby, retired.

Then in 1949 the electrical manufacturing company of Drake and Gorham, Ltd., bought the factory and also the mill, and in the following year transferred the business of a subsidiary company, G. M. Engineering (Acton), Ltd., bringing valuable industry to the town. Switchboards and associated equipment were made there and exported to many parts of the world.

In 1972 Ottermill, Ltd. (as the company was now named) became a member of the giant Westinghouse Group, and the old Georgian factory, although carefully preserved to retain its character, has been greatly extended.

The making of domestic switch-boxes or huge switchboards may seem a far cry from the days when this factory manufactured serges for the East India Company, but it continues to play an important part in the prosperity and life of the town.

Flaming tar-barrels

The annual carnival, which is held on 5 November, is a memorable event and attracts wide interest throughout the West Country. At daybreak the townspeople of Ottery St Mary are awakened by the resounding explosions of the 'rock cannon' being fired at various points of the town, and these startling detonations continue at intervals throughout the day.

The carnival procession takes place in the evening, and comprises a number of tableaux on illuminated floats, drawn through the streets of the town by tractors and lorries. These are headed by the chief marshal, who precedes the carnival queen and her attendants. The guy is carried high, escorted by bearers with flaming torches, and so the colourful procession, accompanied by several bands, goes on its way through enthusiastic crowds.

The bonfires, which blaze on 5 November each year, have a much earlier origin than their association with Guy Fawkes' attempt to blow up the Houses of Parliament. In many cases this custom of lighting large bonfires goes back to the ancient fire-rites performed at the end of the harvest, and what was regarded as the beginning of winter. At Ottery St Mary a gigantic bonfire is built-up in a meadow by the river at St Saviour's. Lashed to a stake at the summit is a chair in which is seated an effigy of Guy Fawkes, and the leaping flames light up the sky for several miles around.

Then follows the event of the evening, known as the 'rolling of the tar-barrels'. For some weeks prior to Guy Fawkes' Day a number of large barrels are soaked inside with tar. Each hotel and inn gives its name to a barrel, and during the course of the evening this is brought out from the inn yard into the street and, after being ignited, is gently rolled from side to side until the tar-soaked interior is well alight. It is then lifted on high by one of the men taking part, and borne upon his shoulders as he careers wildly down the street with fierce flames belching forth from the open-ended barrel. Amid shouts and screams from the onlookers, who scatter before him in all directions, he carries the blazing barrel until relieved of it by one of the other men, who repeats the performance, until eventually the barrel disintegrates, and in a shower of sparks burns itself out in the roadway (see Plate 31).

Meanwhile, the men go on to the next inn where this strange custom is repeated, for during the course of the evening no less than eight barrels make their fiery contribution to the carnival. The 'rolling of the tar-barrels' continues until midnight, and concludes with a sing-song by the remaining revellers, who gather around the dying embers of the last barrel, and the Ottery carnival is over for another year.

The hands of those taking part are well protected by thick gloves made of sacking, and in carrying these heavy barrels some considerable skill and agility is displayed. In the late afternoon there is a boys' barrel, and although this is, of course, smaller, an enthusiastic and impressive performance is demonstrated in Broad Street.

Mention must also be made of the ladies' barrel, which adds to the thrills of the evening, for it is handled with great skill and determination. Woe betide any man who should dare to interfere!

Although attempts have been made from time to time to stop these lively celebrations, they have met with firm opposition from the local inhabitants, which has ensured the preservation of an interesting old custom.

Another custom which goes far back into the past is the proclaiming of the Christmas message. A hand-bell is rung by the 'watchman' outside the church at midnight on Christmas Eve, and the message of peace and goodwill on earth is proclaimed:

> At the Nativity of Christ, Our Lord,
> the Angels did rejoice with one accord.
>
> Let Christmas imitate them here on Earth,
> and crown this day with joy and pious mirth.

This pleasant ceremony is then repeated at various points around the town to herald the Christmas morn, followed by an announcement as to the state of the weather. There was a time when the inhabitants were awakened early on that morning by the rousing strains of 'Christians, awake, salute the happy morn' played by the Ottery silver band.

In more recent times what has become known as 'Pixie Day' has been introduced. This event takes place annually on the Saturday nearest to Midsummer Day, and is devoted mainly to the children. Various sports are organised during the day, and in the evening 'The Pixies Revenge' is enacted in Broad Street. A number of school-children take part as pixies, and after attempting to silence the church bells by capturing the ringers, their evil spell is broken, whereupon they vow to return in the following year to seek their revenge.

The Ottery handbell ringers have become increasingly popular in recent years, and are much in demand throughout the district, especially during the Christmas festivities.

Ottery feoffees

In much the same way as customs and traditions are links with the past, so also are those ancient charities which continue to provide their several needs, as we have already seen in the case of Thomas Axe's Charity (Chapter Seven). Something must now be said about a much earlier charity, which has in recent years been considerably updated.

An inherent philanthropic outlook has for many centuries prompted men and women to give both money and land for the relief of poverty in their own communities, or to provide homes for the aged. Gifts of land for the benefit of the poor gave rise to feoffee charities in many parts of the country, and that of Ottery St Mary must rank among the earliest of them.

The word 'feoffee' is of ancient origin, being derived from the Anglo-French. A feoffee was a person entrusted to hold certain lands, and to apply the rents and profits for relieving poverty in a particular locality. He became 'enfeoffed' or possessed of lands given by generous donors to help the poor.

The earliest record of the existence of Ottery Feoffee Charity is a deed dated 18 January 1440, whereby John Lawrence gave four houses and certain lands in the parish of Ottery to be held by 12 trustees for the benefit of poor parishioners. One of these trustees was to be appointed supervisor and receiver of the rents, which he was directed to put in a wooden chest kept in the church. The chest had three keys, one to be kept by the warden of the collegiate church, another by one of the trustees (feoffees), and the third by a warden of the goods of the church. They were each required to take an oath to keep the chest, all documents relating to the lands, and the monies, for the purposes of the trust, and it was the duty of the supervisor and receiver to render an account of his receipts and expenditure. No more than £40 should be placed or remain in the chest at any time, and the residue should be distributed annually among the poor of the parish where there should be the greatest need and merit.

As will be seen, the original purpose of feoffees was to distribute the income arising from these gifts of land and houses among the deserving poor in their community, and it is interesting to note that payments are still made to certain elderly persons at monthly 'pay-outs'. But as Social Security benefits now meet this need, no further names will be added.

It was natural that in the course of time further lands, and even almshouses, were entrusted to feoffees. Early in the reign of Elizabeth I, six almshouses in Sandhill Street were given by a certain Robert Hone, and placed in the care of the Ottery feoffees. We know little of this Robert Hone, but he appears to have been an Ottery man, and certainly had houses and land there. His daughter, Joan, married John Bodley, an Exeter merchant, and she became the mother of Sir Thomas Bodley, who founded the famous Bodleian Library at Oxford. He was born at High Street, Exeter, in 1545.

About the year 1562 William Sherman, a wealthy Ottery merchant who had then recently purchased Knightstone (*see* Chapter Eleven), founded 12 almshouses in Yonder Street. At the eastern end of this row of houses there was formerly a small chapel for the use of the old people, and Chapel Lane was so named. These almshouses, having fallen into a dilapidated state of repair in 1837, were rebuilt by the feoffees at a cost of £410!

On 17 March 1590 Henry Beaumont by a deed of gift vested property at Ilton, Ashill and Abbots Isle, near Ilminster, Somerset, in the Ottery feoffees for the benefit of the poor of the parish. This formed what was known as 'the 'Somersetshire Trust', but these lands have since been sold and the net proceeds invested or applied towards the cost of providing further flats for the elderly and disabled.

Today there are 22 flats accommodating about 30 people. The Yonder Street almshouses were brought up to modern housing standards in 1972, and re-named 'Sherman House', consisting of 12 flats. On what were originally the gardens at the rear, six ground-floor flats, known as nos. 1–6 Yonder Corner, were built in 1970.

The Sandhill Street almshouses have been demolished and replaced by four modern flats, which were opened in 1974. These are for elderly married couples, and the property has been named 'Robert Hone House' after the founder.

In October 1971, the feoffees provided a day centre in Brook Street to offer recreational facilities to the elderly and disabled of Ottery St Mary and the surrounding district, and light refreshments are obtainable at moderate prices.

The charity is now regulated by a scheme of the Charity Commissioners dated 22 February 1980, which gives the feoffees a wide discretion to meet the needs of the elderly in present-day conditions.

The wind of change

During the post-war years great social changes have taken place, and much of the old character of Ottery St Mary has gone for ever. No longer is it the compact little market town, for new housing estates have spread out beyond the former boundaries, and industrial development has altered the economic structure.

There has been an advance in educational facilities, and a rapid increase in the number of pupils attending the King's School. Extensive and much-needed additions have been made to the school buildings, including a spacious assembly hall (with a stage), a new library, physics laboratory, and domestic science room. In September 1982 this school became comprehensive. A new primary school has also been built in Longdogs Lane.

From those early beginnings with the foundation of the hospital by Mrs. Isabelle Elliot, a first-class medical service has evolved, and in 1982 the enthusiastic enterprise of the local doctors resulted in the building of Coleridge Medical Centre with its computers and most modern equipment. It is a splendid asset to the town.

The long-awaited construction of a link-road, called Canaan Way, has relieved the traffic flow in Mill Street. Proposals for the building of a new fire station (Devon County Fire Service), and the laying-out of pleasure gardens—designated 'an amenity open space'—on the 'land of Canaan', in Hind Street, will add considerably to the amenities of the town.

Although changes come slowly in Ottery St Mary, the trend is towards a steady improvement of facilities. With this expansion there has been a rise in population; particularly was this so during the 1960s, when house-building went on apace.

Under the Local Government Act of 1972 the old Urban District Council was abolished, and Ottery St Mary and the surrounding area was brought within the administration of the newly-formed East Devon District Council with its headquarters at Knowle, Sidmouth.

The continual increase in motor traffic, especially heavy commercial vehicles, frequently causes congestion in the narrow streets, and the provision of adequate car parking facilities presents an ever-growing problem. The town faces a future in which it will have to strive hard to retain its identity.

But it is not the purpose of this chapter to present a detailed account of recent events, for it is only with the passage of time that these may be seen in their true perspective.

Ottery St Mary continues as a busy, thriving town, proudly dominated by its splendid medieval church, which is acknowledged as the finest parish church in Devon, and possessed of a fascinating history going back to Saxon times. In spirit and appearance those vanished ages may seem far removed from our own times, but they are part of our story, and in this very soil are the roots of our heritage. This thought was well expressed by Thomas Carlyle (1795–1881), when he wrote:

> . . . whoever was uprooting a thistle, or a bramble, or draining out a bog, or building himself a house, that man was writing the history of England.

A rich and treasured inheritance has been handed down to us through the years, and it is with confidence and pride that we may look to the future.

The weathercock (*c*.1340) on the spire of the north tower of the church.

NOTES

Chapter One (p. 1)

1. Neolithic or New Stone Age (*c.* 2400–1900 B.C.).
2. An early hillfort with only a single rampart and ditch for defensive purposes.
3. The Celtic name for the river Exe was Isca, which simply meant 'water', and the Dumnonii was the early tribe, which made its centre there before the Romans came.

Chapter Two (p. 4)

1. *per* Sir Frank Stenton.
2. A list of values for taxation purposes.
3. The Saxon charter of 1061 was confirmed by an inspeximus charter (i.e., an attested copy) during the reign of Henry III, and by another of Richard II.
4. Valuable research was carried out by the late Mrs. F. Rose Troup, who read a paper entitled 'The Anglo-Saxon Charter of Ottery St Mary' before the Devonshire Association, 22 June 1939.
5. Proceeding southwards along East Hill to 'Wyrtrum' (an enclosure formed by the upstanding roots of fallen trees), the boundary is approached which divided the manor of Ottery into two estates.
6. O.E. Heafod, meaning 'head'—the upper end of a valley or source of a stream.
7. Harepath: a Roman road suitable for the legions to march along, i.e., an important road. Note, Harepath Hill, near Seaton, Devon.
8. On their journey along the parish bounds the officials, and those accompanying them, stopped at ancient boundary marks, such as particular trees, or prominent stones, wells, and fields, or at those places where they had formerly existed, and then moved on to the next.

Chapter Three (p. 11)

1. Vol. I, folio 104 (*see* Appendix A).
2. A mark was a coin of the value of 13s. 4d. (67p).

Chapter Four (p. 15)

1. The dedication of the high altar at Exeter Cathedral took place on 18 December 1327.
2. Bishop Peter Quivil (1280–91); Bishop Thomas Bytton (1292–1307), and Bishop Walter de Stapeldon (1308–26).
3. Pope John XXII died on 4 December 1334.
4. *Aquebauli* were those persons who carried the vessel of the holy water in processions and benedictions. Scholars in minor orders were generally chosen for this office.
5. Edward III assumed the title of King of France in 1339 in right of his mother, Queen Isabel, daughter of Philip IV.
6. Canon J. N. Dalton in *The Collegiate Church of St Mary* (C.U.P., 1917), expressed the view that St Stephen's chapel may originally have been dedicated to St Gabriel the Archangel and St Anne.

7. *Medieval Carvings in Exeter Cathedral,* by C. J. P. Cave (Penguin, 1953).

8. The plague known as the Black Death reached Melcombe Regis (now part of Weymouth), Dorset, in August 1348.

9. Sir Ifor Evans in *A Short History of English Drama* (Penguin, 1948).

10. This account of the desecration of Bishop Grandisson's tomb is given by John Hooker, Exeter city chamberlain, in his so-called *History of Exeter* (no. 52), written in 1599. It was copied by Samuel Isacke, when he published the printed edition of his father's *The Antiquities of the City of Exeter* in 1677. In 1886 a memorial window was placed at the west end of the south aisle of Exeter Cathedral. The central light represents Bishop Grandisson, whilst on either side are two ecclesiastics holding models of the west front of the cathedral, and the church of St Mary of Ottery.

11. This mandate against the playing of tennis or other games in the churchyard was published on 26 August 1451.

12. Astley, a village near the northern border of Warwickshire, was the home of the Grey family. In 1343 Sir Thomas Astley had built a great collegiate church there. As this college had fallen into ruins by 1608, the chancel was restored and it was converted into a parish church.

Chapter Five (p. 30)

1. These endowments included the appropriations of the benefices of Northam, Ipplepen, and Ilsyngton in Devon, and also *Blossom's Inn*, St. Lawrence Lane, London, and other property, which had been bequeathed with it to the college by Nicholas Braybrook.

2. The only churches still vested in governors are Crediton, Wimborne Minster, Tewkesbury Abbey, and Ottery St Mary.

3. The houses lately belonging to the college were described as 'Le Vikar's house, Le Secondaries house, Le Queristers' house et Le Scole house' with their appurtenances.

4. This was a special court formed by Henry VIII to determine suits and controversies relating to monasteries, and other religious houses and abbey lands.

5. The dissolved Cistercian Abbey of Dunkeswell (*Donkyswylle*), north of Honiton, was purchased by John Haydon in 1539 from Lord Russell for the sum of £28 on condition that he removed the fabric, including all iron, glass, timber, tombstones, and tiles, from the site within 10 years; but the lead was specifically excluded.

6. J. C. Nichols' *Literary Remains of Edward VI* (1857).

7. A pilaster was a flat rectangular column against the screen. At the foot of that on the left of the tables of the commandments was the date 1603, the year of King James I's accession.

Chapter Six (p. 36)

1. Mariansleigh consisted of a cluster of houses set on a high ridge to the south-east of South Molton. The 15th-century St Mary's church was destroyed by fire in 1932.

2. James Gillman, *The Life of Samuel Taylor Coleridge.*

3. Thomas de Quincey, *Recollections of the Lakes and the Lake Poets.*

Chapter Seven (p. 41)

1. A stage-wagon drawn by six horses, one in front of another, was similar to a carrier's cart. The passengers had to make themselves as comfortable as possible on the floor among the softer goods being carried, such as bales of straw. The waggoner was not allowed to drive with reins from the front seat of the wagon in case he should fall asleep, so he had either to walk beside the leading horse, or to ride on an extra horse beside the team.

2. This was towards the end of the year 1634, as the old Roman calendar was still in force, and the year 1635 did not begin until 25 March.

3. Bedford House was situated to the east of the present general post office in Bedford Street, Exeter. It was built by the Earl of Bedford on the site of a Dominican Friary after the Dissolution in 1539, and was used as a town house by successive Earls of Bedford until 1773. This historic house was destroyed during the blitz on Exeter in May 1942.

4. Edward Thomas, *A Literary Pilgrim in England* (O.U.P. paperback, 1980).

Chapter Eight (p. 57)

1. Reverend Daniel Lysons, *A Topographical and Historical Account of Devonshire* (1822).

2. Sydney Smith (1771–1845) referred to the great storm in a speech made at Taunton in 1831, when he stressed the futility of the House of Lords rejecting the Reform Bill.

3. Edward Blore (1787–1879) was royal architect to William IV and Queen Victoria. He was responsible for restoring and partially rebuilding Lambeth Palace. Sir Walter Scott's house, Abbotsford, was designed by him.

Chapter Nine (p. 66)

1. In reply to the question 'Where do you reside?' contained in the diocesan visitation returns for the years 1764/5, 1771 and 1779, the Rev. John Coleridge expressly stated that he did not live in 'the Vicarage House' (as he called it), and wrote 'I reside in the public School House'.

2. Aunt Susannah was a sister of the Rev. John Coleridge.

3. Many years later, when Coleridge was in his early thirties and living in the Lake District, the sound of a calf bellowing one July evening reminded him of this incident. He wrote, 'Instantly came to my mind that night I slept out at Ottery, and the calf in the field across the river, whose lowing so deeply impressed me'.

Chapter Ten (p. 71)

1. The Ottery fire engine was no more than a hand pump. On one occasion, before the telephone was available, a man clad only in his pyjamas had to hurry off on a motor cycle to Exeter to obtain help when a fire broke out at night in Mill Street.

2. Between the years 1795 and 1863 some 712 pupils had attended the King's School.

Chapter Eleven (p. 86)

1. This was the right to dig peat and cut gorse for fuel upon another man's ground.

2. Tristram Risdon wrote this work between 1605 and 1630, but it was not published in full until 1714. He had died in 1640.

3. John Haydon was the second son of Richard Haydon of Woodbury, and came from an old Devon family. His father died in 1521. The Haydons were descended from John Haydon de Boughwood in Harpford parish, who was living there in 1325. The present place-name 'Bowd' would appear to be a corruption of Boughwood, or bow wood, from which bows were made for the archers.

4. It was stated in *A Topographical Dictionary of England*, by Samuel Lewis, published in 1831, that races were held occasionally at Cadhay Lawn.

5. O.E. *hol* meaning 'hollow', i.e., deep, and *cumb*, 'a valley'.

6. On Benjamin Donn's *Map of the County of Devon* (1765) there appears the description 'Remains of a Chapel' at Holcombe.

7. Anthony Woodville (or Widville), who was possibly a cousin of Thomas Grey, Marquess of Dorset, unsuccessfully laid claim to Knightstone as next heir of the Bittlesgates.

8. Henry Grey, third Marquess of Dorset, created Duke of Suffolk, was beheaded on Tower Hill on 23 February 1554.

APPENDIX A

THE DOMESDAY BOOK ENTRY (tom. i. fo. 104) relating to Ottery

Ecclesia S. Marie Rotomag. ten. de rege Otrei. Ipsa Ecclesia teneb. tempore regis Edwardi et geldabat pro xxv hidis. Terra est xlvi car. In dominio sunt iii car. et xvii servi et lv villani et xxxiiii bord. cum xl car. Ibi v porcarii redd. xxx sol. et xv den. Ibi iii molini reddentes xxx solid. et cc acr. prati et viii Hide pasture et xx acr. silve et unum Hortum et i salina reddens xxx denar. in Sedemude terra S. Michaelis.

See Chapter Three, page 11.

Notes

(1) A hide of land was the English unit, being as much as could maintain one family, or as much as could be ploughed by a single ox-plough. It varied from 40 acres to 120 acres, according to local usage.

(2) A carucate or carve of land was about 100 acres of arable land, or as great a portion of land as might be tilled in a year and a day by a single plough.

(3) Servi were bondsmen or servile tenants (labourers).

(4) Villani or villeins (villagers) were men of servile condition, bound to the manor for life. They were small peasant farmers.

(5) Bordarii (bartoners, or borderers) were possibly boors, husbandmen, or cottagers, each having a bord or cottage with a piece of land held in return for produce. They were of a less servile state than the villeins.

(6) Swineherd was a man who tended the pigs on the swine-pasture.

(7) Sedemuda (Sidmouth); *see* Appendix D.

APPENDIX B

WARDENS OF THE COLLECIATE CHURCH OF ST MARY OF OTTERY, 1337–1545

1337/8	January 17	Richard de Gonisale	Appointed provisionally (Commendatory Warden)
1338	June 24	Richard de Otry	Succeeded on this date
1350	May 9	Henry Bonet	Resigned on this date
1350	June 17	Andrew Attemore	Succeeded on this date
1379		John Coterel	Name occurs in records
1397		William Slade	Succeeded in this year
1399	October 17	John Bokeland	Admitted on this date
1412		John Tyrel	Died late in 1414
1415	January 28	John Sarger, M.A.	Succeeded on this date
1446	August 31	John Hancock, M.A.	Admitted on this date
		Thomas Stephens	
1490	December	Thomas Cornysh	Suffragan Bishop under Hugh Oldham, Bishop of Exeter (1504–19). Died in 1531. Buried in Wells Cathedral, Somerset
1511	June 27	Thomas Mitchell	Succeeded on this date

Appendix B—Wardens of the collegiate church of St Mary of Ottery—*cont.*

1513	October 9	Thomas Chard	Suffragan Bishop under John Veysey, Bishop of Exeter (1519–51).
1518	October 16	Walter Dudman, M.A.	Wardenship confirmed on this date
1525	June 26	Oliver Smythe, M.A.	Vicar of Ipplepen, and Ilsyngton. Subscribed to Henry VIII's Supremacy on 13 July 1534
1544	October 30	John Ffysher	Appointed warden by John Veysey, Bishop of Exeter (1519–51); Surrendered on 28 May 1545

APPENDIX C

EARLY VICARS OF OTTERY

1154 to 1189	William Roger	Vicars of Otrei in the reign of Henry II as recorded in the Registers of the Cathedral Church of St Mary at Rouen
1191	Peter the Clerk	Resigned in this year
	Roger the Chaplain	Succeeded
1283	John de Wolfrington	Implicated in the murder of Walter de Lechelade, precentor of Exeter Cathedral on 9 November 1283.
1297	John de Middleton	
1310	Gulfridus	Died in this year
1310	John de Thormerton	Required to reside in the parish
1329 to 1331	John de Sharnebok	Instituted on 17 October 1329 contrary to the patron's right to appoint. Revoked by Letters Patent under the Great Seal on 22 January 1331
1335	Oliver de Fayrsy	Collated on 21 April 1335. He was the last vicar before the foundation of the college

THE COLLEGE OF ST MARY OF OTTERY founded on 22 January 1337/8

See Appendix B: Wardens of the collegiate church, 1337–1545
(Dissolution of the college on 24 December 1545)

VICARS OF OTTERY ST MARY

1550	John Bagster	
1580	Ralph Mainwarynge, B.A.	Became vicar of Sidmouth and also Aylesbeare on 22 January 1612. Buried 30 July 1635.
1590	Nicholas Forward	Succeeded on 2 November
1626	John Forward	Succeeded to 'the office of his father'.
1660	Melchizedeck Alford	Became vicar on 20 March (*see* Chapter Seven)
1691	William Hull	
1692	John Rost	
1694	John Burrows	
1695	Thomas Gatchell	Buried in chancel of Ottery church on 17 July 1713
1713	Hugh Lewes, M.A.	
1713	Richard Jenkinson	Died in February 1721
1722	Ralph Farthing, B.C.L.	Became vicar on 24 April

Appendix C—Vicars of Ottery St Mary—*cont.*

1743	Richard Holmes, M.A.	Became schoolmaster 1731, chaplain priest 1738, and vicar on 26 May 1743
1760	John Coleridge, B.A.	Schoolmaster (appointed on 20 August 1760); became vicar on 27 December 1760. Died suddenly on 6 October 1781 (*see* Chapter Six)
1781	Fulwood Smerdon, B.A.	Became vicar on 21 November 1781. Buried in Lady Chapel of the church on 7 August 1794, aged forty
1794	George Smith, M.A.	Became vicar on 5 December 1794
1841	Sidney William Cornish, D.D.	Master of the King's School from 1824 to 1863. Became vicar on 18 November 1841
1874	William Henry Metcalfe, M.A.	
1890	Maitland Kelly, M.A.	Canon
1900	William Emmanuel Pryke, M.A.	Canon
1908	John William Metcalfe, M.A.	
1920	Leonard Bristow Stallard, M.A.	
1938	Bernard Cecil Jackson, M.A.	
1950	David Rufus Price, B.A.	
1978	Peter John McGee, M.A.	Became vicar in January 1978; prebendary in November 1982. Team rector (Otter Vale Team Ministry) in February 1983.

The advowson or gift of the living of Ottery St Mary remained vested in the crown until 1870. It is now held by the Bishop of Exeter.

APPENDIX D

LOCAL PLACE-NAMES

ABBREVIATIONS

Celtic (or British): 300 B.C.–A.D. 650
O.E. Anglo-Saxon (or Old English): A.D. 650-1066
D.B. Domesday Book (1086)

Alfington	.. ..	the farmstead (-tun) of a Saxon leader called Ælfa and his family, i.e., 'the farmstead of the Ælfings'. The connecting link -*ingas* indicates 'the family of . . . '
Allerbeare	.. ..	(O.E: alor, -bearu), 'the alder wood or grove'
Awliscombe	.. ..	(Aulescome, D.B.) (O.E. awiell, source of a river or stream; -cumb, a valley.) 'The valley where the stream has its source'
Axminster	.. ..	(O.E. esce, water; mynster, monastery.) 'The abbey by the water (river Axe)'
Axmouth	.. ..	(O.E. esce—from Celtic, Isca; -muda.) 'The mouth of the water, i.e., the river Axe'
Aylesbeare	.. ..	'the woodland clearing (O.E. -bearu) of a Saxon leader named Ægel'
Beer	.. .. ..	A clearing in woodland or marsh (O.E. -bearu). Common in the South-West; there are over 100 examples in Devon. Originally spelt 'Bere', e.g., Bere Regis in Dorset
Bowd	.. .. ..	(Boghewode, 1281; or Bowood.) A wood where bows were made—'curved wood'
Branscombe	.. ..	(Brancescumb, c. 1070.) The narrow valley. (O.E. -cumb) taking a Celtic personal name Brannoc, i.e., 'Brannoc's valley'

Local Place-Names—*cont.*

Broadhembury	..	'the Great fort' (referring to the nearby Iron Age hill-fort known as Hembury Fort—O.E. Heaburg, 'the high fort'). 'Broad' is used here in the sense of meaning 'great' for the purpose of distinguishing the the village from Payhembury (q.v.)
Budleigh Salterton	..	(Saltre, 1210.) (O.E. sealtere, a salter), 'the settlement (O.E. -tun) of the salt-workers'. Salterton was a small place within the manor of Budleigh, where salt-making was carried on in the salterns, or salt-pans, along the margins of the estuary of the river Otter, which was wider then, but later silted up
Cadhay	..	Land enclosed by a hedge (O.E.[ge]haeg or hege), which was occupied by a Saxon thane named Cada. It was 'Cada's enclosure'
Clyst, river ..	..	Celtic in origin. Possibly means 'the clean stream'
Colyton	..	(Celtic 'cul', meaning 'the narrow one'), 'the farmstead or settlement (O.E. -tun) by the narrow stream'
Colyton Raleigh	..	The farmstead of a Saxon named Cola and his followers. 'Raleigh' was added in Elizabeth times
Colyford ..	..	'the crossing-place over the narrow stream'
East Budleigh ..		Personal name Budda combined with O.E. -leah, 'the clearing in the wood made by Budda', i.e., Budda's glade or woodland clearing
Exeter		(Escanceaster, 876; Execestre, D.B.) O.E. Esce, derived from the Celtic river-name Isca ('water'), followed by O.E. -ceaster (Latin, castra, a fortified camp). 'The Roman town on the Exe'
Exmouth ..	..	(Examuda, 1072), 'the mouth (O.E. muda) of the water', i.e., at the estuary of the river Exe
Fairmile	..	'le faire mile', which probably meant a good stretch of the Roman road to Exeter (now the A.30) at a time when roads were generally little better than rough tracks, and frequently very muddy
Farway	..	(Farewei, D.B.) (O.E. faer, -weg, meaning 'a way'), 'the frequented road'—an ancient track across the greensand plateau
Feniton	..	'the farmstead by the fen or marsh (Vine Water)'
Gittisham ..	..	(Gidesham, D.B.), possibly 'Gyddi's village (O.E. -ham) by a stream'
Gosford	..	(Goseford, 1249; Gosford, 1330), 'the goose ford'. The place where geese crossed the river Otter
Harpford ..	..	Originally Hareford, 'the ford or crossing-place carrying an important highway' (O.E. Herepaeth, an 'army path'). This was the old Roman road from Dorchester (Durnovaria) to Exeter (Isca Dumnoniorum), and suitable for the Roman legions to march along
Honiton	..	The settlement (O.E. -tun) of a Saxon leader named Huna and his people, i.e., 'Huna's farmstead'.
Larkbeare ..	..	the wood or grove (O.E. -bearu) frequented by larks, i.e., 'Larks' wood'
Metcombe ..	..	'the meadow (O.E. maed) valley (O.E. -cumb)'
Newton Poppleford ..		'the new settlement (O.E. -tun) by the pebbly ford (O.E. popel) or crossing-place over the river Otter. A 'popple' was the Devon name for a pebble or round stone. Harpford (q.v.) was the earlier settlement
Northleigh		the north clearing in a wood (O.E. -leah)
Otterton.. ..	..	'the Saxon settlement (O.E. -tun) by the river Otter'
Ottery St Mary	..	(O.E. oter, meaning otter, with the final syllable O.E. ea, meaning 'water or stream.') 'The place by the Otter-stream.' Anglo-Saxon settlements in the valleys often took their names from the rivers near which they stood
Payhembury ..	..	'the place near the high fort (O.E. Heaburg)'. Possibly named after a Saxon thane called Paega

Local Place-names—*cont.*

Plymtree	(O.E. plym, meaning plum, and -treow, a tree.) A plumtree in pastoral fruit-growing country
Rockbeare	(Rochebere, D.B.) 'Rooks' wood' (O.E. -bearu)
Salcombe Regis ..	the valley (O.E. -cumb) where salt was worked, i.e., 'the salt valley'. The Domesday Book (1086) records that there was a saltwork at Sidmouth nearby
Seaton	the Saxon settlement (O.E. -tun) by the sea (O.E. Sae)
Sidbury	'the fortified place (O.E. -burg) in the broad valley', taking its name from the early Iron Age hill-fort to the south-west of the village
Sidford	'the crossing-place over the stream in the broad valley.' *See* Sidmouth
Sidmouth	the mouth (O.E. -muda) of the broad valley (O.E. sede, meaning 'the broad one'), as distinct from the deep narrow valleys, such as Branscombe, Dunscombe, Weston Combe, and Salcombe
Sid, river	a river taking its name from the broad (O.E. sede) valley through which it flows
Slade	(O.E. slaed.) A low flat valley or dell
Southleigh	the south clearing or open space in the wood (O.E. -leah)
Talaton	the Saxon farmstead (O.E. -tun) by the swift stream (Celtic, tala, meaning 'the swift one')
Taleford	the crossing-place over the swift stream. *See* Talaton
Tipton St John ..	the farmstead (O.E, -tun) of an Anglo-Saxon named Tippa and his followers. St John was a much later addition.
Topsham	Saxon personal name coupled with O.E. -ham. 'Topp's riverside land.' Possibly had an earlier name
Whimple..	a Celtic place-name. Possibly meaning 'the white pool'.
Wiggaton	the farmstead (O.E. -tun) of a Saxon chief named Wicga and his followers, i.e., 'Wicga's farmstead'
Woodbury	the fortified place in the woods (O.E. wudu, -burg), being near the Iron Age hill-fort known as Woodbury Castle
Venn Ottery	(Fenautre, 1575), 'the fen or marshland by the river Otter'

A SELECT BIBLIOGRAPHY

An Account of the Church of Ottery St Mary (Exeter Diocesan Church Architectural Society, 1842

Bates, Darrell, *The CompanionGuide to Devon and Cornwall* (1976)

Cameron, Kenneth, *English Place-Names* (1961)

Coleridge, E. H., *Coleridge Poetical Works* (Oxford, 1967); *Letters of Samuel Taylor Coleridge* (1895)

Coleridge, Lord, *The Story of a Devonshire House* (1905); 'The History of the Town of Ottery St Mary' (a lecture delivered in 1897)

Cornish, S. W., *Short Notes on the Church and Parish of Ottery St Mary, Devon* (Exeter, 1869)

Dalton, J. N., *The Collegiate Church of St Mary* (Cambridge, 1917)

Dickinson, F. B., *A Lecture on the History of the Church of St Mary of Ottery* (Exeter, 1897; sixth edition, 1953); 'Our Parish Registers' (a lecture delivered in 1898)

Ekwall, Eilert, *The Concise Oxford Dictionary of English Place-names* (Oxford, fourth edition, 1960)

Griggs, E. L., *Collected Letters of Samuel Taylor Coleridge*, six volumes (Oxford, 1956–72)

Holmes, G. E. T., *The King's School. A History* (1963)

Hoskins, W. G., *Devon* (1954); *The Making of the English Landscape* (1955); *Two thousand years in Exeter* (1960, reprinted 1979); *Devon and its People* (Exeter, 1959)

Little, Bryan, *Exeter and its Surroundings* (1953); *The Monmouth Episode* (1956)

Ottery St Mary Parish Register, 1603-1839, two volumes (Exeter, 1908-29)

Polwhele, Richard, *History of Devonshire* (1797–1806)

Raine, Kathleen, *Samuel Taylor Coleridge: A Selection of his Poems and Prose* (The Penguin Poets, 1957)

Reader, W. J., *Life in Victorian England* (1964)

Rose-Troup, F., *The Great Fire at Ottery St Mary, 1866* (Exeter, 1936); 'The Anglo-Saxon Charter of Ottery St Mary' (a lecture; proceedings of the Devonshire Association, 1939)

Slader, J. M., *The Churches of Devon* (Newton Abbot, 1968)

Whetham, C. D. and M., *A Manor Book of Ottery St Mary* (1913)

Whitham, J. A., *The Church of St Mary of Ottery* (Gloucester, eighth edition, 1982)

INDEX

119